TREASUR

OF BLESSINGS

brian@threetowers.co.uk

TREASURY OF BLESSINGS

The Servants of Christ the King
1943–2014

BRIAN BRIDGE

© The Servants of Christ the King, 2015

Published by: The Servants of Christ the King

Website: www.sck.org.uk

A CIP catalogue record for this book is available from the British Library.

ISBN 978-0-9935553-3-6

Book layout and cover design by Clare Brayshaw

Prepared and printed by:

York Publishing Services Ltd
64 Hallfield Road
Layerthorpe
York YO31 7ZQ

Tel: 01904 431213

Website: www.yps-publishing.co.uk

CONTENTS

PREFACE

In mid-1995, about to go away on holiday, I received a large envelope containing a bundle of leaflets and papers describing a body I had never heard of before: the Servants of Christ the King (SCK). I glanced at a few of the leaflets, thought they looked quite interesting, and put them aside to read later. Needless to say, there was a mass of other correspondence to catch up with when I returned from holiday, so it was several weeks before I got around to re-opening the envelope. I was astounded to find a covering letter which I had not spotted before, inviting me to become Warden of SCK. So I read the leaflets more carefully! It became clear to me that if SCK was what it was claimed to be I should give serious attention to this invitation. So I replied, asking to meet some members and to experience the SCK way of waiting on God. This was duly arranged. I met SCK as it really was and I was not disappointed.

I was a Quaker at that time and it turned out that my name had been put forward to SCK by someone at Friends House, the headquarters of Quakers in Britain. I was known to some there as not only an active Friend but also a former Anglican who had revived his sacramental links with that church. I was minded to accept the invitation. I took my thoughts on this to a clearness meeting, a Quaker practice not dissimilar to SCK's way of 'waiting on God', though intended to help towards discernment on personal rather than corporate decisions. I was appointed Warden of SCK in January 1996.

During the next three years I presided at SCK conferences and visited local groups around Britain. I encountered some remarkable people and many examples of Christian love and service. I also met a widespread anxiety about the future of SCK, which was numerically in decline but very precious to those who remained. I began to understand just how and why SCK was regarded as such a treasure.

When I was first beginning to learn about the Servants of Christ the King I was given a copy of *An Adventure in Discipleship* by Roger Lloyd (Lloyd, An Adventure in Discipleship, 1953). Written by the founder and first Warden of SCK, this book set out the theology behind the movement and told the story of the first ten years. It has been out of print for many years, though many second-hand copies are still in circulation. Another book describing the experience of SCK, *The New Commandment: The Servants of Christ the King* by Olive Parker (Parker, The New Commandment, 1962) is also out of print. Both books are in some important ways outdated. Many of their examples of Christian action are far removed from what would be relevant or even possible in the twenty-first century. But the basis of SCK is, put simply, to wait on God together in whatever situation a group finds itself and to obey the divine imperative if and when that is discerned. This has lasting validity.

The idea of a new book first came to me in 2007. At first it was going to be a new edition of *An Adventure in Discipleship* with an extended preface bringing the story up to date (Bridge, Revision of 'Adventure in Discipleship', 2008). But as I began to explore the SCK archives it became apparent that much more than a preface would be needed. Not only had there been many developments since 1953, but there was much even in the earlier years which needed further explanation or critical reflection. The archives held a treasury of writings by SCK people, providing material for a better understanding of the whole project. It was enlightening to go back to original versions of some leaflets which SCK had re-edited and re-published over the years. I began to think of bringing out an anthology of these writings, letting them speak for themselves.

But by 2012 it was becoming apparent that SCK as a movement sustained by voluntary effort was ageing and losing energy, and would not be able to go on much longer. If a new book was to be written, it should be SCK's legacy for those who would come after. I was greatly encouraged by Wendy Robinson, the last Warden of SCK, who saw both the need and the opportunity. Paradoxically, the end of SCK as we knew it could be exactly the right time for understanding what it was all about. As Roger Lloyd once wrote:

> The difficulty of describing living movements is that they are always changing and cannot be precisely plotted and pinned down. That they are perpetually in motion is evidence of the life in them. It is only when

they are dead that they achieve tidiness of form and finality of shape. (Lloyd, The Cell Movement and the Servants of Christ the King, 1949)

So I came to know that I had to write this book, drawing on the riches of the past but adding an appreciation which is only possible with a certain amount of distance and hindsight.

The annual conference, Central Company and trustees of SCK have been a constant support ever since I first brought the idea to them. I wish to thank all those members and former members of the Servants of Christ the King who have helped me in the writing of this book. Many have contributed their memories and some have given me previously unpublished and unarchived papers retrieved from their garages and attics. When I have needed to check the facts I have always been able to turn to Lance Haward, whose commitment to and detailed memory of SCK have enabled me to fill many gaps and to understand the context of the many accounts which have been given to me.

I have benefited greatly from the helpful comments of readers of the draft text: Tim Brooke, Alison Norman, Ella Simpson and Sandra Heavenstone. They have spotted mistakes and omissions and have helped me to think about the structure of the book. Any faults which remain are entirely mine.

Lambeth Palace Library is the home of the SCK archives. There I have spent happy hours, always meeting with unfailing helpfulness. I intend that the papers which I have accumulated from other sources shall be deposited there in due course. I have been received with kindness and much help at the Hampshire Record Office in Winchester, which now holds the archives of the Dean and Chapter of Winchester Cathedral; and at the Senate House Library of the University of London. I have consulted many books, including most of the published works of Roger Lloyd, the founder of the movement. I hope that the present book with its bibliography and index will make the life of future researchers a little easier. The index has been expertly prepared by Sarah Wilson of Cressing Indexing.

I have learned to give attention to the physical readability and durability of the book, which are essential if it is to have a long and productive life. I thank Daniel Edwards and Nicola Barnacle for opening up my mind to the world of book design, and York Publishing Services for helping to turn these ideas into the reality which you are now holding in your hands.

This is the story of a movement which for over seventy years gave inspiration and encouragement to many and diverse people and supported them in their work for the world and their care for one another. I believe that SCK deserves to be known not only in this generation but in times to come, when the needs for community, common concern and concerned action will be no less apparent. I pray that this book will not be found too inadequate an expression of the vision.

Finally I would like to thank my wife Rosalie for her unfailing patience and support, without which *Treasury of Blessings: The Servants of Christ the King 1943-2014* would never have come to fruition.

Brian Bridge
London, August 2015

INTRODUCTION

Founded in 1943, the Servants of Christ the King (SCK) soon became a fellowship of fellowships with groups around the English-speaking world. Over the years the movement adapted to a changing church and a changing world, yet always kept its essential character. Its members met in small autonomous groups to wait on God in an alternation of prayer and discussion, seeking to become people whom God could use, affirming the indivisible bond between contemplation and action. The formal organisation of SCK came to an end in 2014, though some local groups continued to meet. The experience of the movement and its local groups ('companies') provides much material for reflection on right relationships between prayer and Christian action, between personal and corporate discernment, and between small committed lay groups and the wider church.

The original vision of the founders of SCK was of an Anglican lay order to work for the evangelisation of English society, reaching people whom the English parish system had been unable to touch. SCK companies in factories and offices, waiting on God for their inspiration and sensitive to local needs, would become leaven for the making of a Christian society. These companies would be bound together by a minimal national organisation but would act in obedience to their local Anglican churches. They would work quietly, with no publicity. Members would make a promise for one year at a time to live by a strict rule of devotion and fellowship, which, however, would not preclude them from continuing in their working and family lives.

The designation of SCK as an order was soon dropped and the hoped-for growth of groups in places of work was never realised. The evangelisation of England by this or any other means later came to be questioned as a valid aim in a changing society of many faiths and none. But SCK companies continued to meet and to wait on God in the way which they had undertaken from the beginning, open to be guided into whatever corporate vocation might open to them. Over the years the features with which SCK began were modified one by one until almost all had changed, with the exception of the essential practice of waiting on God. Because SCK was willing to go wherever it was led by this prayerful dependence, the movement was able to continue moving on. This practice was described in my booklet *Waiting on God: Seeking God's Calling Together in Small Groups* (Bridge, Waiting on God, 2013).

The present book records the challenges faced by the movement and reflects on what happens in practice when real people try to live out this kind of commitment. Part I consists of five chapters tracing the pre-history and history of SCK in more or less chronological sequence. The seven chapters of Part II contain reflections on key aspects of the life of SCK, including waiting on God, common concern, small groups and the 'fellowship of fellowships', with a final chapter summing up what SCK has meant during its seventy-year life. The book incorporates many quotations from writings by Roger Lloyd, Olive Parker, Alison Norman and other SCK people, as well as records of decisions made by the conference and Central Company. Part III reproduces in full three documents which I regard as so significant that piecemeal quotations cannot do them justice. All of these documents are about the SCK practice of waiting on God. The first is almost certainly by Roger Lloyd, the second by Edmund Morgan and the third by Gonville ffrench-Beytagh.

SCK has left its mark on those who have known it, including myself. SCK was not simply a formula or even a vision. To be sure there was and still is a formula – waiting on God in a structured pattern of prayer and discussion. There was once a mission – the Christianisation of England through the quiet working of small groups waiting on God. But the original mission was never fulfilled and no formula alone can account for the deepening of fellowship, love and service which was so remarkable and remarked in those who had met with the SCK experience. I hope that this book will serve all those whose lives were touched by SCK as a reminder of the blessing which they have received. For those who never experienced SCK but who long for that blessing of fellowship, love and service there are some pointers here, and possibly some warnings too. Committed small groups like all human organisations have their dangers. If SCK was preserved from the worst of these, it was by God's grace. To God be the glory.

A note on style

In the interests of consistency I have made some changes in spelling and punctuation, both in the passages quoted in the body of the book and in the appended texts. I have not, however, ventured to impose consistency of wording on my sources. For example both 'waiting upon God' and 'waiting on God' will be found in quoted passages, even though I am told that 'upon' is out of favour these days and have avoided it myself.

PART I

THE STORY

CHAPTER ONE

A NEW ORDER

The Servants of Christ the King took shape in Britain in the middle of the Second World War, a time of deep moral and social concern. On all sides people were asking: 'What kind of world are we fighting for?' If this was to be a world with Christian values, what were these values, how were they to be embodied in society, and how were they to be spread when evangelism seemed largely to have failed?

On 26th May 1942 a letter went out from the Cathedral Close in Winchester to 160 members of the Church of England around the country, both lay and clerical, up to and including the Archbishop of Canterbury, William Temple. The author of the letter and the proposal which it introduced was Roger Bradshaigh Lloyd, Canon of Winchester. But the concern was not his alone. A small group of clergy had chanced to meet at a conference in January of that year and with the addition of one more member it was this group which commissioned Roger Lloyd to write the proposal on its behalf. Roger Lloyd identified the members of this founding group in an article written in 1951:

> ... the four archdeacons (as they were in 1943: they are now the Bishops of Edinburgh, Truro, Malmesbury, and the Archdeacon of Northampton) who, with me, were primarily responsible for starting SCK ... (Lloyd, The Future of SCK, 1951)

This statement makes it possible to put names to the five founders of SCK. They were Kenneth Warner (1891-1983), Edmund Morgan (1888-1979), Ivor Watkins (1896-1960), John Grimes (1881-1976) and Roger Lloyd (1901-1966). The four who were archdeacons in 1943 held those posts in Lincoln, Winchester, Bristol and Northampton respectively.

The full title of the proposal was *A Design for an Active Religious Order of Anglican Laity for the Purpose of Providing the Church of England with an Organised and Disciplined Body of Witnesses* (Lloyd, Design for an Order, 1942). The opening paragraph read:

> In October 1939 Mr. T. S. Eliot's very impressive book *The Idea of a Christian Society* was published. Its chief purpose was to suggest the goal of a nation deliberately Christian in its organisation, its social institutions, and its culture, and to help its readers to think more clearly about what such a goal means in itself, and about the steps which Christians could take which might lead there. ... If [the individual] is to be fully redeemed, and to be made at last an heir of the full Christian liberty, the society, as a unit, must also be redeemed. The community and the individual are both objectives of Christian evangelism. (Lloyd, Design for an Order, 1942)

The proposal went on to list problems faced by Christian evangelism in England at the time: 'a vast, unwieldy, and apparently unyielding mass of ignorance of and indifference to religious truth' in the general population, and 'an angry scorn of all the churches, more particularly the Church of England' even among students and others who were in principle welcoming to religious truth as such.

> But side by side with all this, there also exists a wider realisation than there has been for many years past that the Christian social principles and the Christian valuation of individual personality are inextricably embedded in the frame of the Christian supernatural view of life; and that all this is not only relevant to the freedom and the peace of the world, but a necessary condition of it. (Lloyd, Design for an Order, 1942)

From this it was concluded that Christian evangelism had to go out into communities and in particular into the world of work.

> The church has a social and industrial duty to discharge, a mission to communities, trades unions, trading concerns, and every other kind of organisational unit. This is not less and not more important than its acknowledged mission to separate persons one at a time. Thus, a church which neglects to define and perform its duty to communities cannot today speak the word of God with authority to individual souls. (Lloyd, Design for an Order, 1942, p. 2)

However, this was seen as being beyond the capabilities of the parochial system, which was 'much better at shepherding a static population than they are at evangelising a mobile people'. Something more was needed:

> We have to bring the Gospel into these communities as communities, into Broadcasting House and Unity House, and, without a vast expansion of our present methods, we cannot do it. The material of this expansion can be drawn only from our congregations. ... The spearhead of the new evangelistic army must be found among the workers, the teachers, the works managers, they themselves bearing witness in the places and the conditions where they work. (Lloyd, Design for an Order, 1942)

A new Order was proposed to bring these people together within the Church of England. The Order would be co-ordinated on a national scale, 'wide enough in scope and membership to make its appeal to every type of Christian to be found in our congregations', and anchored within parishes of the Church of England but not tied to one form of churchmanship. This body of trained, disciplined and devoted people dedicated to Christian witness would go into the many fields of modern life which were out of reach of clergy but in which Christian laity had a footing. Its purpose would be to recruit a sufficiency of believers for the building of a Christian England. Although the detail of what the Order was to do would have to depend on performance,

> [it] includes activities so various as intercessory prayer; the offering of all kinds of secular service in the name of the Lord; direct argument to convince the doubter and convict the sinner; the power of attraction implicit in any congregation which means business by its faith and shows it in the quality of its worship, and the mental effort put into the social planning of a Christian England by those who have the necessary specialised knowledge – all these and many more besides. And as all these adventures are seriously undertaken by groups of Christian laymen in all parts of the country, they fit into each other because they are all directed towards the same end, a Christian England. (Lloyd, Design for an Order, 1942)

The new Order was to be a religious society to which people would be drawn by a sense of vocation. It must not be merely an organisation for social service under a religious title, even though the witness of social service would come within the range of its task. The Order would have groups and not individuals as its units.

The individual members of a group within the society must learn to pray together and to help each other to a truer knowledge of God and a wider ability to receive and use his grace. Their spiritual devotion must constantly reinforce and underline their witness or their witness will fail. In the group it ought to be impossible to say where their prayer ends and their work begins. To this end the group would have to meet regularly, and the first obligation of a member would be that of regularity in attending the meetings of the group. The group would meet to pray, to survey the possibilities of witness in its area, to make some report of the work done since it last met, and to draw up a programme of witness for the next period. The second obligation, therefore, is that of obedience to the decisions of the group, just as the group must obey the broader decisions of the Order as a whole. (Lloyd, Design for an Order, 1942)

The paper concluded with consideration of the relationship between the proposed new Order and the parish church, expressing the hope that 'each group of the Order would regard the vicar as a kind of prior, and that he, in his turn, would regard them and their leader as the spearhead of his evangelistic work'. Safeguards were proposed to avoid the risk that the Order would ever operate in a spirit of independence of, or even of hostility to, the parish church:

[I]t is clear that this relationship will have to be carefully guarded and defined, and when it comes to writing a constitution the following points might probably be included: (1) No group in any parish without the written goodwill of the vicar and church council. (2) Before a member can be admitted, he must be vouched for by his vicar. (3) The wider organisation of the Order to follow diocesan lines; and the whole to be under the supervision of a bishop, and an advisory council appointed by (perhaps?) the Church Assembly. (Lloyd, Design for an Order, 1942)

Some of the influences which led to *Design for an Order* were mentioned in that document and its covering letter. For others we have to look to the earlier writings of Roger Lloyd, to memories of the time, particularly those recorded in *An Adventure in Discipleship* (Lloyd, An Adventure in Discipleship, 1953), and to what we can learn of the interests and experience of the group which commissioned the writing of the proposal.

The opening paragraph of *Design for an Order* referred to *The Idea of a Christian Society* (Eliot, The Idea of a Christian Society, 1939). This book, based on a series of lectures given by T. S. Eliot at Cambridge in

March 1939, called for and delineated a society whose basis would be Christian: 'not a society of saints, but of ordinary men, of men whose Christianity is communal before being individual'. In such a society the great majority of people would belong to one church, which in this country would be the Church of England. Eliot had declared himself to be a 'classicist in literature, royalist in politics, and Anglo-Catholic in religion' (Eliot, For Lancelot Andrewes: Essays on Style and Order, 1928). His deep concern for Christian community was shared by other Anglo-Catholic thinkers at the time, though most of these were well to the left of Eliot in politics.

Roger Lloyd wrote in *The Spectator* in 1940 of the 'kind of dream' of Christian politics in a Christian polity, without which there was no hope for England or for Europe. He associated that dream in England with the thinking of J. H. Oldham, T. S. Eliot, John Middleton Murry and Christopher Dawson (Lloyd, The Way to a Christian Policy, 1940). It would appear from the article that Roger Lloyd did not know that these people were in active association with one another. In fact all except Dawson (the only Roman Catholic among them) were meeting more or less regularly in a group called 'The Moot' which Oldham had convened in 1938. This group also included Gilbert Shaw (Hacking, 1988, pp. 61-2), who attended the founding conference of SCK in 1943 and became priest-adviser to an SCK company of students at King's College London. In their different ways, both Eliot in *The Idea of a Christian Society* (Eliot, The Idea of a Christian Society, 1939) and Middleton Murry in *The Price of Leadership* (Murry, 1939) had recognised the importance of local communities within the larger community. A Christian society could not be built from the top down. But the community which attracted both Eliot and Middleton Murry was a rural one, whereas Roger Lloyd was looking to where power lay, instancing the daily paper, the municipal orchestra (!), the town council, the Federation of British Industries, and the Miners' Federation. (Lloyd, The Way to a Christian Policy, 1940)

Roger Lloyd had been active in the Industrial Christian Fellowship when serving as a young curate in the Manchester diocese while William Temple was Bishop of Manchester (Lloyd, The Industrial Christian Fellowship, 1925). He remained on close terms with William Temple right up to the death of Temple in 1944, as their correspondence shows. The tone of the Archbishop's letters to Roger Lloyd is friendly, the salutation is invariably 'My dear Roger' and the valediction 'Yours ever'. The 1941 Malvern Conference on the Life of the Church and the Order of Society was called and chaired by William Temple, who was then Archbishop of York. Speakers included T. S. Eliot, Dorothy L. Sayers, Maurice B. Reckitt,

John Middleton Murry, V. A. Demant and H. A. Hodges. Many of these were associated with the Anglo-Catholic Summer School of Sociology and with the Christendom Group (Lloyd, The Church of England 1900-1965, 1966, p. 310). Among those present at the conference were Archdeacon Kenneth Warner, soon to be one of the founders of SCK, and several others who became SCK members or priest-advisers. The findings of the conference were published by the Industrial Christian Fellowship and the papers were published separately later in 1941 (Archbishop of York's Conference, 1941).

The conclusions of the Malvern conference became known as the Malvern Declaration (Archbishop of York's Conference, 1991). In the letter sent out with *Design for an Order* Roger Lloyd stated that the new kind of lay Order proposed

> [is] the kind of thing which I imagine the Malvern Conference had in mind when it recommended the formation of an Anglican Third Order for lay evangelism. (Lloyd, Covering letter sent with *Design for an Order*, 1942)

The reference was to section 10 of the Malvern Declaration. Headed 'The Community Life of the Church', the opening words were:

> The church as we know it does not manifest this life of true community. We, therefore, urge that enterprises be initiated whereby that life can be made manifest. (Archbishop of York's Conference, 1991)

It continued with a call for action at three different levels. The Church of England as a whole was to reorganise its own economic and administrative system; at parish level the whole congregation was to meet regularly to plan and carry out some common enterprise; and 'cells' were to be formed on the basis of common prayer, study and service. Finally,

> The church might further encourage the development of ways and means, whether through membership of a Third Order or otherwise, which would enable men and women to live under a definite discipline and rule whilst following the ordinary professions of life. (Archbishop of York's Conference, 1991)

Writing ten years later, Roger Lloyd related that one of the original group of four 'was impressed by the cell movement, then in its infancy, though he believed that if these cells were to be really effective they must be obedient to some discipline, and that they must somehow be joined together so as to make some pastoral oversight possible'. Another member of the group 'had had much experience of the power of small groups, and had himself been one of the pioneers of the way of reaching decisions by the use of a corporate waiting upon God' (Lloyd, An Adventure in Discipleship, 1953, p. 26). The addition of Edmund Morgan to the group strengthened the link with the cell movement further. He was a founder member of the 'Fellowship in the Gospel' formed in 1937 under the leadership of Reginald Somerset Ward (Ward, 1937) (Morgan, Reginald Somerset Ward: His Life and Letters, 1963, pp. 34-5) (Beach & Beach, 1981, p. 62). He started a cell in the Winchester diocese for prayer for the work of SPG (Beach & Beach, 1981, p. 64) (Anon., Personal impression of the first meeting of the cell, 1937) and was listed as a member of the Advisory Group for Christian Cells when it was set up in 1940 with the approval of Archbishop Cosmo Gordon Lang (Advisory Group for Christian Cells, 1940).

Design for an Order envisaged that the primary unit of the Order would be the local group, consisting of between four and twenty people, bound together in prayer, with each person committed to regular attendance at meetings and obedience to group decisions. There was no mention of how decisions were to be reached. The rule of unanimity which would become so important for SCK may have been in the minds of the founders, but was not explicitly mentioned.

The proposal elicited a strong response. Questions were raised about some of the details, particularly the relationship between the Order and the parochial system, but a large majority felt that this was something which had to be taken forward. Roger Lloyd toured the country sounding out how such an Order might be received in the Church of England as a whole. Two experimental groups were set up, in Brierfield near Burnley and in Cambridge. Finally it became clear that the proposal was ready to be moved on another step. Fifty people of great diversity were invited to a conference, which was set to take place at St Hugh's College, Oxford in January 1943.

* * *

The founding conference had five days, from 3rd to 7th January, to do its work. But, as Roger Lloyd later recollected:

> Never in my life have I seen a conference in such an apparently hopeless tangle as we were on the eve of Epiphany, 1943. It was Margaret Cropper who then saved us by suggesting that we should scrap all we had done so far, and spend the whole morning of the

Epiphany in silence, waiting upon God. (Lloyd, SCK Newsletter, 1948, p. 1)

After that, everything moved forward at an astonishing pace. It was agreed that a new Order should come into existence, initially for an experimental period of one year. The lay people at the conference drafted a constitution and the clergy reduced sixteen previous drafts of a rule to one in the space of a single afternoon. On the following morning, the last morning of the conference, the constitution and rule were unanimously approved. Only the name of the Order remained to be decided. Various suggestions had been put forward in advance, including 'The Order (or Society) of Saint George', 'The Christian Commandoes' (sic), 'Christian Action', but all were found wanting. It was only in the final hours of the conference that someone suggested 'The Servants of Christ the King' and this found general approbation.

The decisions of the conference were set out in a founding statement entitled 'An Order for Anglican Laypeople'. It opened with a prayer and a statement of faith:

> O God, we pray for the Servants of Christ the King, that thou wouldst count us worthy of our calling and fulfil in us all the good pleasure of thy goodness and the work of faith with power: that the name of the Lord Jesus Christ may be glorified in us and we in him, according to thy grace.

> God is the creator of the universe and his plan for the world is made known and made possible by Jesus Christ, who wills to win, to save, and to guide men and women by means of the community of Christians commonly called the church. (SCK Conference, 1943)

The purpose of the new Order was to help the Anglican church towards the 'renewal of the corporate sense' which was needed if she were to fulfil her mission. With this in view, the Order would seek to establish companies of dedicated, committed, trained and disciplined Christian lay people, whose aims would be:

> to fulfil their lives in obedience to Christ through the discipline of the Order; to strengthen the reality of common membership in the body of Christ, by witness of the fellowship of the Order; to draw others to Christ and his church; and to help towards bringing the spirit of Christ into the working of social, industrial and political life and so to claim all the powers of society for the kingdom of God. (SCK Conference, 1943)

The unit of the Order was not to be the individual member but a company of not less than three and not more than twelve Anglican laymen and laywomen. During the experimental year companies would consist of enquirers and probationers, since full membership had to be preceded by at least a year of probation. Full membership would wait for a tested conviction that it was God's will for the person to join the Order; enquirers would be seeking to know whether this was God's will for them; probationers would be testing their conviction. Each company was to choose by unanimous vote from among its own number a company leader whose duty was to secure the proper conduct and the regularity of the meetings. A priest-adviser, appointed by a diocesan representative with the consent of the company, would have powers of veto over company decisions.

Two kinds of companies were envisaged, parochial and vocational. A parochial company would be formed wholly from the congregation of a parish church, and would have that parish as its common concern. It could start only with the consent and goodwill of the incumbent. Members of vocational companies on the other hand would be drawn from a non-parochial and vocational sphere such as 'the home, the business, the factory, the club, the institution, etc'. A vocational company should aim to start companies in the parishes from which the members came, though not necessarily themselves joining such companies. Conversely, members of parochial companies should aim to start vocational companies.

The rule which was adopted laid down three obligations arising from the belief of the individual member that he or she had been called to serve God in a company of this Order:

> To worship at least once a week in church, however difficult that may be, to receive Holy Communion regularly and frequently, to spend a definite time daily in prayer and bible reading, and to learn ever more of the Christian faith.

> To seek through the company to which I belong, and through every means in my power to draw others into the fellowship of the Church, and to claim for the rule of Christ every part of human life, both in my country and throughout the world.

> To be a loyal member of the Anglican Communion in that province and diocese in which I live, and to be obedient to the unanimous decisions of my company in the Order. (SCK Conference, 1943)

So the Servants of Christ the King were on their way, though with aims and structures which would soon become barely recognisable in SCK as it developed. Some of the later changes were in response to events which did not turn out as expected. Others were developments of what had been latent in the first initiative, or clarifications of what had been in the founders' minds all along but taken for granted and never made explicit. What was soon to be recognised as the life and the soul of SCK was mentioned in only one brief paragraph in the interim constitution and rule:

> The whole foundation of the life of the company is corporate prayer, and waiting upon God in a due alternation of discussion and prayer, in the belief that God will make his will known. (SCK Conference, 1943)

The next seventy years of SCK's existence can be seen as an expansion of these few words.

CHAPTER TWO

AN UNDISCLOSED PURPOSE

It was soon found necessary to clarify and develop the commitment to 'waiting upon God in a due alternation of discussion and prayer'. During the course of 1943 a leaflet was sent out to all SCK companies, with the title *Waiting upon God*. It began:

> We have now reached the stage where companies are springing up in various parts of the country. ... Now in order that we should all relate our prayer and work to the one common purpose, it seems right that from time to time every company in the Order should pray and discuss and seek to know the will of God in just the same way as every other company. (Anon., Waiting upon God, 1943)

The leaflet went on to describe 'a tried and tested form and way', with a cycle of prayer and discussion consisting of silent prayer, controlled discussion, free discussion, further silent prayer, discussion and testing of unanimity, making the record, and offering the record. The leaflet, probably written by Roger Lloyd himself, added: 'By this means, the company will eventually arrive at a decision about what its own evangelistic purpose is, and also how it is to attempt to fulfil it.'

Another significant feature of SCK which may have been clear to the founders but did not appear in either *Design for an Order* or the statement of the founding conference was the principle of no publicity. This was simply put into practice: from the first, SCK leaflets were marked 'For Private Circulation only and not for Publication'. It had already been in Roger Lloyd's mind in 1941 when in his notes for a meeting of the Winchester Fellowship he wrote of the danger of publicity as 'the besetting temptation to this offering of life':

By announcing a programme we are saying publicly that we know what God wants done. We emphasise human rather than divine initiative. Such publicity commits us to doing something. If it isn't done it's bad for morale; on the other hand by being committed to 'doing something' we are often driven to act ahead of God to save face. There is always lurking round the corner our own desire to be noticed and to enhance our reputation. (Lloyd, Notes for Winchester Fellowship, 1941)

Despite the 'no publicity' principle, Roger Lloyd was able to write about the early experience of SCK in his book *The Inspiration of God* (Lloyd, The Inspiration of God, 1944, pp. 37-40). After asserting that 'the special grace which we call inspiration ... is normally bestowed through consecrated communities', he went on to describe, though without naming, small cells of convinced lay Christians who were bringing the challenge of the gospel to communities 'such as Broadcasting House, the House of Commons, the government youth club, the great aeroplane works' and training themselves in a devotional response to God's initiative in order to receive his inspiration for the work to which they were called. Their meetings consisted of a combination of prayer and discussion, using 'a technique ... which a process of trial and error in a good many such groups has now made clear'. A description follows of the rules governing the prayer, the discussion and the decision, which together make up the practice of waiting on God. The groups or cells should be bound together in 'a wider community, a sort of lay Order for Christians ready to live out their Christianity in this kind of way'. The description is clearly of the Servants of Christ the King though the name is not given, and must have been written in 1943, since the designation as a 'lay Order' was dropped at the beginning of 1944.

* * *

By the beginning of 1944 there were forty companies of the Servants of Christ the King. The second annual conference was held at Epiphany 1944. Roger Lloyd reported the decisions of the conference in the SCK Newsletter:

The purpose of a conference is to decide things, and the material on which we had to work was the experience of our companies during the first experimental year of the life of the Servants of Christ the King. The main piece of experience was the conviction that waiting upon God is indeed the characteristic way, the life and the soul of

SCK but together with that came the evidence that a good many of our companies were experiencing some difficulty with its use. Therefore we began with a full explanation of it by the Bishop of Southampton. (Lloyd, SCK Newsletter, 1944, p. 4)

The newly appointed Bishop of Southampton was Edmund Morgan. His explanation of waiting on God was soon to be printed as a leaflet and circulated to all SCK companies (Morgan, Waiting upon God: An Explanation, 1944).

The conference unanimously agreed that SCK should continue, but not as an Order:

> The important change which the conference made was the unanimous if rather regretful agreement to drop the word 'Order'. This was done chiefly because, as we all believed, it was God's will for us at this stage of our life. There seemed to be no doubt that to retain the word meant that we were moving into a morass of complication and difficulty over the whole question of the promises and obligations of full members. There are not ten per cent of us who could undertake any addition to the actual rules either of SCK as a whole, or of the particular company. The change from probationership to full membership is to be marked by a solemn dedication in church, to be renewed annually, and in a searching form of words which will in future be the preamble to the General Rule. (Lloyd, SCK Newsletter, 1944, p. 4)

If SCK was no longer an Order, then what was it? No designation – 'society', 'movement', 'fellowship' or any other – was found adequate to take its place. It was simply 'The Servants of Christ the King'. In later years SCK came to be described as a movement, though not without misgivings, since companies were so diverse and their concerns so varied.

SCK companies had originally been for lay people only, though each company had a clerical adviser. Now unofficial experiments were to be allowed with separate companies consisting entirely of clergy. Youth companies were also allowed on an experimental basis.

Although it may not have been apparent at the time, the SCK which emerged from the 1944 conference was no longer bound by the aspirations of its founders as expressed in *Design for an Order* (Lloyd, Design for an Order, 1942). By putting the practice of waiting on God at its very centre, SCK recognised that any group which wishes to be obedient to the inspiration of the Holy Spirit must be prepared to let go of its presuppositions and to give its first attention to learning to be people whom God can guide.

Design for an Order had envisaged local parochial and vocational groups, each working in its own way but towards a single end, the Christianisation of England. At the foundation of SCK and for some years thereafter it was expected (at any rate by Roger Lloyd) that every company would have an evangelistic purpose. By waiting on God they would find what that purpose was and how they might fulfil it. Great hopes were set on the growth of vocational companies, which were to permeate or infiltrate the secular world, including factories and other places of work.

The hope that SCK companies would spring up in factories was not realised except in a very few cases. Companies flourished mainly in parishes where there was a sympathetic incumbent. Such 'vocational' (non-parochial) companies as existed were mainly in colleges and universities. SCK was not being used in the way which the founders had envisaged. These concerns were considered in five days of prayer and discussion at the SCK annual conference in August 1948. Although the aspiration for vocational companies was not dropped, the conference declared that 'history had declared the will of God for us' and that the first mission of SCK was within the Church.

> This we believe because the demands of membership in an SCK company are such that they can be met only by those who are already regular and praying members of the Church, and living its full sacramental life. We are sure we must not weaken those demands, nor forsake our Anglican basis. If this, our conviction, is true, it follows that while we welcome gladly every kind of vocational company, our chief aim at present must be to increase the number of the parochial companies and to use them where possible as a step to the formation of vocational companies. (SCK Conference, 1948)

The growth of SCK companies in Anglican parishes was now to be encouraged by easing the no-publicity rule and by trying to persuade clergy that SCK companies would be an asset to them in their work. Christian evangelism in workplaces was seen as best carried out by non-denominational cells, which could be initiated or supported by SCK 'ambassadors' but which would not themselves be part of SCK. Finally, SCK members were reminded of the need for greater sensitiveness in all relationships with the people around them, and urged to a renewed effort in 'steady and imaginative intercession'.

William Temple was invited to address the 1945 conference of SCK but died suddenly on 26 October 1944. His support had been crucial for the beginnings of SCK and Roger Lloyd had kept him briefed on the movement as it developed. We can only speculate on how things might have gone on if he had lived longer, but it is clear that his death was a great loss both to the movement and to Roger Lloyd personally.

As it turned out, the conference scheduled for April 1945 had to be cancelled because the intended venue became unavailable. Instead, a smaller 'executive conference' was held in Winchester to deal with some outstanding problems. Roger Lloyd's account shows that the course set by the 1944 conference had not yet been universally accepted:

> There are, as I said, two matters for decision which cannot wait until 1946. The first is whether our particular way of corporate waiting upon God ought to continue to be what it is now, an obligation laid on every company, or whether it ought to be voluntary. One of the advisers' conferences in the summer came strongly to the conclusion that it should not be an obligation. This is clearly a matter of great importance, and we must decide it; and in any case, the fact that it has been raised at all shows that, however it is decided, the activity of waiting upon God needs more explanation, and training too, than has so far been given. The second question to be answered is, has the time come when we may allow ourselves greater freedom in self-propagation, in spreading SCK, than we have thought it right to enjoy in the first two years of our life? And if so, how much freedom, and how can we define what steps we may or may not take? With demobilisation looming ahead it is plain that this whole question must be thought out again, and either the old policy of 'No Publicity' reaffirmed, or a defined modification of it arrived at. (Lloyd, Cancellation of Conference, 1945, pp. 2-3)

The executive conference reaffirmed both the centrality of waiting on God and the policy of 'no publicity'. It called for the 1943 leaflet *Waiting upon God* (Anon., Waiting upon God, 1943) to be completely rewritten. This was quickly done, probably by Roger Lloyd himself. (Anon., Waiting upon God, 1945)

The 1948 conference decided that it was time for a leaflet about the Servants of Christ the King to be written by a layman. The draft was ready by November and was approved by an inner circle of original co-founders of SCK consisting of Roger Lloyd, Edmund Morgan, Ivor Watkins and John Grimes. The name of the author is not known. The group which approved the leaflet decided that it should be published privately and should not be reviewed in the church papers. It was duly printed with the words 'Not for Publication' prominently displayed on the front cover. Its availability was announced in the SCK Newsletter in February 1949.

It is not clear how far it was distributed beyond those who were already members of SCK companies, or whether such limited publication and avoidance of notice in the press were what the conference had had in mind. The leaflet was an excellent statement of what SCK stood for at the time, written with clarity and real joy. (Anon., The Servants of Christ the King, 1949)

If the 1948 conference had hoped for growth in the parishes, it did not come. There was disappointment that SCK seemed not to be living up to its purpose. Roger Lloyd returned to the theme in an SCK Newsletter article in 1951.

> Is all well with our companies? Is all well with the leadership and the organisation of the movement? Are we doing all that we really might do, under God, for the work of evangelism? Some companies, almost certainly, have almost ceased to function. Others, but always for good and sufficient reasons, have recently disbanded. On the other hand, there are other scenes in the whole picture, at Ipswich, for instance, in China, and Swindon, and elsewhere, where the most scrupulous examination reveals nothing that one could desire to be different, and everything for which to thank God. (Lloyd, The Future of SCK, 1951)

Although the article was entitled 'The Future of SCK', it did not propose a change of direction but only an organisational overhaul. There had already been some administrative changes, including the setting up in 1950 of a Central Company to share decision-making with the Warden and Secretary. However, Roger Lloyd felt that companies needed more help from the centre by way of visiting and shepherding to which he was not able himself to give enough time. He announced a special 'domestic conference' to be held in Oxford in January 1952 to answer these questions and to make decisions about the future.

* * *

In the event, Roger Lloyd was prevented by illness from attending either the 1952 Oxford conference or the preceding Central Company meeting whose preliminary findings were intended to help the conference to get down to its business. This may have been a hidden blessing. As a member of the Central Company wrote afterwards:

> The absence of Canon Lloyd ... has proved once and for all that SCK is indeed a creation of the Holy Spirit to meet the needs of our present age, and is not dependent either upon its Warden or original founders or any particular group of its members. ... Without a priest

in their midst, and with two not originally of their number, the Central Company found itself experiencing to the full the fact that the Servants of Christ the King is a movement particularly for the laity, and in which all its members are equal. (Anon., Oxford Conference, 1952)

The conference tried to ease the load on Roger Lloyd by changing the role and structure of the Central Company. It was now to include representatives from each region and to take on much of the responsibility for nurturing SCK companies. The conference declared that the main work of SCK lay within the (Anglican) church, at least for a while ahead. Roger Lloyd later commented on the decisions of the conference, reiterating his view that evangelism was the main purpose of SCK but recognising that the church was not yet prepared for it.

Until the church is a home of peace and mutual love, until we all know what the gospel actually is and why it is as fully a gospel to the twentieth as to the first century, and until we learn to rely more fully on the inspiration and the power of the Holy Spirit, the church is still in the phase of being prepared for evangelism. We have still far to go before the Church of England is the instrument the Holy Spirit can use to the full for the conversion of England. (Lloyd, Message from the Warden, 1952, p. 4)

The newly reconstituted Central Company lost no time in getting down to its work. It had to address both the need for companies to be nurtured and sustained and the heavy workload which this had placed on Roger Lloyd and his Secretary. Roger Lloyd had complained that the number of companies was not growing. The Central Company, after waiting on God, came to the conclusion that the no-publicity rule had to go. SCK had to come out into the open. The unveiling was to take the form of a book, which the Central Company commissioned Roger Lloyd to write. This was hardly a reduction in his workload, but at least he could work from home, and in a medium in which he was comfortable.

An Adventure in Discipleship: The Servants of Christ the King (Lloyd, An Adventure in Discipleship, 1953) came out in July 1953. It was Roger Lloyd's twentieth published book. It received good reviews in the national and church press. Sales exceeded expectation. A second impression was needed in the first year. By February 1954, sales had reached over 5,000 copies (SCK, 1954). The book went into a third impression in 1955 and was still selling at a rate of 400 copies a year in 1959 (SCK Central Company, 1959). SCK and its way of waiting on God were now set before the public. Within less than a year of its publication three new and eight or nine potential companies were attributed to it, as well as an increase in membership of several existing companies. Yet *Adventure in Discipleship* was hardly designed as a means of recruiting new members. No contact address was given in the book, and even the fact that Roger Lloyd was a Canon of Winchester Cathedral was not mentioned, though it had appeared on the title page in practically all of his other books. The nearest to a modest invitation came in the preface by Edward Wynn, Bishop of Ely, who wrote that 'perhaps some who read will be called to join with them in the work' (Lloyd, An Adventure in Discipleship, 1953, p. 5).

A medical student at an English university was already involved in groups preparing for and assisting a university mission. Someone gave her a copy of Roger Lloyd's book. She and some fellow-students read it and formed a company to wait upon God, following the method as described. Unknown to them, there were already three SCK companies in the same city. The little group continued until the students reached their finals and then disbanded as they went their several ways. It was only after two years that the former student, Pauline Haswell, learned that Roger Lloyd was a Canon of Winchester Cathedral and wrote to him there. By this roundabout means she eventually came into the wider SCK, just before setting out for work in Africa as a mission doctor. Later she was to help start SCK companies in three continents.

Another reader of the book was inspired to try the method with other worshippers at her parish church, 'until we found that we had become a company of Servants of Christ the King' (Parker, The New Commandment, 1962, p. 11). She was Olive Parker, who was within a few years to become the Secretary of SCK and played a major part in its development. Others who first encountered SCK through *An Adventure in Discipleship* included Peter Thorburn and Gonville ffrench-Beytagh, both future Wardens of SCK.

The publication of *An Adventure in Discipleship* introduced the method of waiting on God to a wider range of Christian people. The 1948 SCK conference had already agreed to a partial relaxation of the no-publicity rule to enable members to spread SCK and its principles. The main obstacle and the main target of persuasion was seen as the reluctance of many clergy to have SCK companies in their parishes. Now lay people as well as clergy were able to read for themselves and to consider whether they were called to this form of corporate prayer and action. Some groups formed in this way came into the wider movement of SCK, but we shall never know how many groups started and continued without any connection to others who were doing the same.

Nevertheless the number of known SCK companies remained obstinately small. New companies were started but others lost their enthusiasm and gave up after a few years. Six years after the publication of *An Adventure in Discipleship* there were still fewer than 120 companies in Britain, with perhaps at most a thousand members in total. Roger Lloyd tried to address the question of why so many were unwilling to join. In an article entitled 'Is SCK Excessively Spiritual?' he reflected on the statement by a regional conference held in Edinburgh that there was 'a real danger of potential members being alarmed by the degree of spirituality which seems to be required of them in SCK'. He began by confirming that many people had expressed misgivings about the demands of SCK membership, quoting from correspondence which he had received: 'I'm not good enough for this' – 'My people aren't spiritually advanced enough to take on a thing like this' – 'Somehow it all frightens me'. He identified three features of SCK life which might be putting people off: silence, vocation and the rule. In response to these anxieties he did not propose any change in SCK practice, but pleaded for better explanation and teaching. The understanding of vocation which SCK had reached was difficult to explain, but expressed what Roger Lloyd considered to be 'a clear and definite piece of biblical theology'.

> A Christian's orders come from God through the Holy Spirit. It is for us to ask for orders, it is for God to give them. Sometimes we can tell quite clearly what they will be, but much more often we can't. Further, God cannot very well give his orders to any group of people until he sees that they are ready to carry them out. They must first become teachable and usable. Therefore we first have to offer ourselves for whatever purpose it shall please God to use us, and only very seldom do we know in advance what that purpose is. In fact, we accept a vocation to an undisclosed purpose. Even then, God seldom discloses the whole of his purpose for us at once. We are shown one step at a time. We must take the first step. When we have done so, but not before, we are allowed to know what the second step is. In all this, there is nothing peculiar to SCK. If Christians mean anything whatever by the phrase, 'relying on the Holy Spirit', then something like this is what they must mean. Where SCK comes in is here, that our corporate company life provides the shelter and the setting within which, and the method by which, it is more possible for us than otherwise it might be to know God's will, and even to hear the whisper of his voice. (Lloyd, Is SCK Excessively Spiritual?, 1955)

A further attempt to promote SCK was made in a new leaflet published in 1960. This was written for distribution in churches and provided a contact address for enquirers. Entitled *In Company Together*, it presented SCK and its companies as an approach to Christian living.

> They are learning to know and trust each other on a deeper level than is possible in most casual acquaintance with one's fellow church folk. They are discovering a little more of the meaning of fellowship in Christ. As in a happy human family, they get to know each other's faults as well as each other's good points and to love and trust each other just the same. (SCK, 1960, p. 1)

The leaflet went on to describe the process of waiting on God as a way of making decisions in the light of God's holiness and truth.

> A company finds out what work it has to do by waiting upon God. ... In each case, the important thing is that the members are learning to grow and to work together. Each one is gradually forgetting his likes and dislikes and his self-importance and learning to give freely of his talents and opportunities to a common cause. (SCK, 1960, p. 3)

Examples were given of the work of companies in Britain and overseas, including missions, supporting house churches, work with children and young people in parishes, supporting a prison chaplain, and bringing people of different races together in the church life.

The main emphasis of *In Company Together* was on the fellowship of the company in 'a pattern of prayer, discussion and action where each plays his part and appreciates the value of the others'. However, there was no direct appeal to the reader to form a company or to join an existing one. The invitation was to write to the Secretary 'for any details you would like or for any help you think SCK could give'.

* * *

Roger Lloyd resigned as Warden of SCK in 1961 because of concern about his wife's health. He remained influential in SCK, corresponding and speaking at conferences right up to his sudden death in 1966. His successor as Warden was Richard Hamilton Babington, Archdeacon of Exeter. Born in 1901, the same year as Roger Lloyd, he had been a vicar in the Winchester diocese until 1942 and was closely involved in the discussions which led to *Design for an Order*. In that year he had moved to Ipswich as Vicar of St. Mary-Le-Tower. A whole chapter of *An Adventure in Discipleship* was devoted to the Ipswich experience

(Lloyd, An Adventure in Discipleship, 1953, pp. 107-119). Two of the earliest SCK companies were formed there. Later, when SCK was facing the apparent failure of vocational companies as a means of evangelism, Richard Babington invited Roger Lloyd to address a meeting of all the clergy of the Ipswich area. From this came the formation and growth of a clergy company with a common concern for what came to be known as 'permanent neighbourhood mission', and from this in turn came the development of lay SCK companies which were to bring in the resources of all the local congregations. The Ipswich clergy company not only provided the continuing support for the mission, but was also a training ground for priest-advisers for the lay companies. By 1953 there were ten lay SCK companies in and around Ipswich (Lloyd, An Adventure in Discipleship, 1953, p. 112).

The new Warden had been involved in SCK from the very beginning. Roger Lloyd admired his approach to evangelism and his vision of how SCK companies could contribute to local evangelistic effort. Nevertheless there were signs of change. In 1959 the Central Company had put out a statement recalling companies to 'their primary concern for evangelism' and reminding them that 'our prayer, discipline and fellowship are the means of spreading the kingdom of Christ and not ends in themselves' (SCK Central Company, 1959, p. 1). But by 1963 Richard Babington was able to write of waiting on God as 'surely an end in itself and not just a means to an end' (Babington, Waiting upon God, 1963). Change was on the way and Olive Parker, who had been the Secretary of SCK since 1958, was to be one of the instruments of that change.

CHAPTER THREE

OPENING THE DOORS

From 1961 onwards there was a steady stream of SCK publications, some aimed at wider publicity, others intended for leaders and existing members. *In Company Together* (1960) was followed by a shorter leaflet dating from 1962, simply entitled *S.C.K.* and apparently aimed at bulk distribution in churches. Five reference cards came out in 1961, respectively entitled *The Committed Group*, *The New Life in Action*, *What Does a Company Do?*, *How Companies Start*, and *Practical Notes on Conducting a Session of Waiting on God*.

Olive Parker's book *The New Commandment* was published by Darton, Longman and Todd in 1962 (Parker, The New Commandment, 1962). According to the cover blurb, it was 'no attempt to recruit new members for an organisation, but a means of sharing the opportunities and joys that have come the author's way in the course of her work as secretary of the movement'. Although Olive Parker was a less experienced author than Roger Lloyd, her book was well written, clear and systematic. The descriptions of company life and particularly of the annual SCK conference were lively and realistic. *The New Commandment* provided a fuller treatment of theological principles and of the General Rule than *Adventure in Discipleship*.

The statements of theological principles were largely consistent across both books, but Olive Parker took them in the order of fellowship, Spirit, mission – the exact reverse of the order adopted by Roger Lloyd. This was perhaps an indication of the point which SCK had now reached. Its founders had clearly seen it as an instrument for evangelism, but experience and reflection had taught some hard lessons. Being had to come before doing, so the first thing was to become people whom God could use. The way to being made useful, after which a company might be drawn to specific concerns and tasks, was through patient waiting on God in self-offering fellowship. But at its inception SCK was offered to God, 'offered blind' as Edmund Morgan had put it (Rudd, 1960, p. 6), and this could and did lead in directions which could only with difficulty be recognised as evangelism. The mission was 'to become more evidently the firstfruits of the new unity in Christ' and to serve others in whatever ways seemed right in that unity (Parker, The New Commandment, 1962, p. 28).

Although the no-publicity principle had been relaxed with the publication of *An Adventure in Discipleship* in 1953, a certain reticence seems to have lingered on. Olive Parker made her own views clear:

> [W]e seem to have moved into a somewhat uneasy attitude of mind when some of us know that we hold in our hands the way that unlocks the treasures of the kingdom. It is a way that can be walked by any, of any age or kind or intellect. Yet we are inhibited from sharing it with others even when we feel it is most needed through a strange reluctance. ... Are we so careful to preserve the sense that people must be called into SCK that we hesitate to use any pressure on another person? Are we afraid of detracting from the loyalty to the church of God by setting up a lesser loyalty within it? The relevant question to ask is this – How dare we maintain that we hold a key to new life in the church while at the same time tucking it away out of sight of those who may be longing for it? (Parker, An Essay in Self-Examination, 1963, p. 8)

If the SCK way was nothing less than a restoration of apostolic values within the church, it could not be treated as an optional extra to parish life and individual spirituality. The original reticence and avoidance of publicity would have to go, and it would be the duty of the movement and of every company and every member to propagate the SCK way of waiting on God throughout the church. This conviction led to a great increase in the production of literature and advertising, but also to a relaxation of some of the disciplines which might be a deterrent to potential members.

Not everyone was comfortable with the opening up of SCK and the 'propaganda' (Olive Parker's own word) which went with it. Writing several years later, Guy Parsloe, a long-standing member of SCK, reflected on his estrangement from SCK which had set in around this time.

> I am convinced it was an essential part of the vision which launched SCK that its members should embrace a life of spiritual poverty, to serve unseen and unrewarded even by the satisfaction of seeing results. The rule against publicity was probably intended as a defence against adulterating membership with shallow, immature recruits; if so, it must

be judged effective. But it subjected those who did join to a restraint almost unbearable in an age which condemns reticence and a desire for privacy as anti-social and in which an enterprise which fails to expand as fast as the economy inflates is thought to be on the way out.

SCK grew quite fast in the first two or three years; that is, the number of companies grew, though not usually the membership of established companies. Then we became conscious that growth had stopped. We discussed the reasons for this and collected all the 'difficulties' experienced by individual enquirers. Inexperienced in the management of societies, we took the common sense but erroneous course of making entry easier. At the same time we scrapped the 'no publicity' rule. So far as I can recollect, the effect on our numbers was negligible, and I am certain that for me and others the atmosphere of SCK meetings began to be distasteful. (Parsloe, 1971)

The drive for publicity was at least in part a response to a feeling that something must be wrong if the number of SCK companies was not growing. There were varying estimates at the time, perhaps because some companies were semi-dormant and others did not send members to the annual conferences of SCK or were not in regular touch with the SCK office. But even the highest estimate of 150 companies in 1962 amounts to less than one SCK company to a hundred Church of England parishes. Moreover, although some new SCK companies were still being formed, there was a tendency for older companies to lose heart and drop away. Olive Parker referred in *The New Commandment* to the loss of the sense of expectancy, so that meeting as a company became an end in itself. This had the seeds of death in it (Parker, The New Commandment, 1962, p. 32). She returned to the theme of dropout in 1963:

A disturbing fact about company life is that it seems to deteriorate as time goes by. The feeling of adventure and expectancy dies down and is often replaced by anxiety as to what the company should be doing, if anything, and frustration because it seems impossible to get new members. People come into the movement eager for the new life it seems to offer them. Do those who have been in companies for some time give this impression or are they apt to feel that there is a lot in this SCK idea, but they are not sure what? (Parker, An Essay in Self-Examination, 1963, p. 5)

Could anything be done about this falling away of companies? There was much heart-searching about this among those who felt responsible for SCK as a whole. The Central Company had been reconstituted back in

1952 to include regional representatives, with the expectation that they would help to nurture companies in their local areas. But the bulk of this work fell on the Warden and Secretary, who were already giving what time they could to travelling around the country visiting companies and encouraging new groups. A Sub-Warden, Michael Clarke, was appointed in early 1963 to join the 'permanent staff' (as Richard Babington called it). A former headmaster of Repton School, he had been ordained in 1939. He was appointed Rector of Marylebone Parish Church in 1945 and later became Provost of Birmingham Cathedral. In 1947, while Rector of Marylebone, he was described in the *Church Times* as being the London secretary of the Servants of Christ the King (the first mention of SCK in that and possibly any newspaper). By 1963 he was the incumbent of a country parish and chaplain of a school in Gloucestershire. His work in SCK was to be primarily pastoral. Companies were invited to call for help when they needed it. Richard Babington wrote:

> There is no system of visitation or inspection for SCK companies. This is largely due to a strong conviction we have that the government of each company lies in its own deliberations in consultation with the priest-adviser. We are always delighted to have invitations to visit a company and much the same system prevails as in meeting new people. ... While it is true that the adviser is the right and only person to advise, it may be that consultation with someone from outside might be of value from time to time. He would not be in day-to-day touch with the issues that concern a company but could bring the principles of waiting on God and the practice of life in fellowship to bear on the company life. We would like to think that such help could be of service to the adviser as well as to the company members. Perhaps the fact that we have added another priest to the 'staff' will encourage companies to use us in this way. (Babington, Company News, 1963, p. 17)

* * *

This was a time of great change in society in Britain and world-wide. Britain was still in the later stages of the end of empire. Youth culture was being taken seriously for the first time: the Beatles would receive their MBEs in 1965. Sexual and gender norms were being questioned. The debate over the Wolfenden Report of 1957 would eventually lead to the decriminalisation of male homosexuality by the Sexual Offences Act of 1967. Betty Friedan's book *The Feminine Mystique* was published in

1963, providing some of the impetus for 'second-wave feminism'. A new urgency had been given to concern for the environment by Rachel Carson's *Silent Spring*, published in 1962.

The church was also experiencing much controversy and change. The second Vatican Council was in progress, having opened in October 1962. In Britain there was a great debate in the national press and elsewhere around John A. T. Robinson's book *Honest to God*, published in March 1963, which had argued for a secular theology for the twentieth century and questioned the exclusive claims of church and religion. Anglican-Methodist conversations were in progress, raising the hopes of some for a step towards church unity and causing people in both of those churches to think hard about what was essential in their faith. The charismatic movement was stirring. Michael Harper, formerly a curate at All Souls, Langham Place, left that post in 1964 to start the Fountain Trust with the purpose of the renewal of the historic churches. Other charismatic developments were taking place outside the traditional churches altogether.

SCK was also going through a time of reappraisal, provoked not only by outside changes but also by self-doubt and disappointment with the spiritual state of its companies. This reappraisal was undertaken both at the centre and also in regional gatherings. The exercise undertaken by the Central Company was described by Olive Parker, writing in autumn 1963:

> The Central Company has entered a year of self-examination. There are two residential meetings before our next conference in August 1964. At the first in November it will survey the role of SCK in the church today and its relation with kindred movements and societies. At the second in May 1964, it will try to examine how best the movement can be equipped to fulfil this role. We hope that we can arrive at Swanwick next year with some definite suggestions to replan our organisation to produce greater efficiency. (Parker, An Essay in Self-Examination, 1963, p. 7)

SCK had been a purely Anglican body from the start, with a strong emphasis on parish loyalty. As recently as 1962 Olive Parker had recorded that, although some had called for a change to an interdenominational basis, the overwhelming conviction of the movement as a whole was that the fellowship within SCK must be sacramental (Parker, The New Commandment, 1962, p. 31). However, this was now again being questioned. Alison Norman wrote:

How can we, as a denominational cell movement, give effective service outside our parishes? The founders of SCK envisaged companies in hospitals, factories, big industrial concerns and fields of specialised social service, composed of Anglicans seeking to apply Christian principles to the common problems of their working life. But in fact, SCK seldom got off the ground in a non-parochial setting and the reason seems to be that Christian action in professional fields means working with any other Christians you can find. Practising Christians are likely to be few and far between and they can only hope to make themselves effective by working together. If, therefore, SCK is to make any effective contribution outside the parishes, we have to rethink radically its denominational organisation. (Norman, SCK Newsletter, 1964)

The case for interdenominational cells in the workplace had been recognised by SCK as far back as 1948, but at that time these were thought of as separate from, though potentially supported by, SCK companies. Now the proposal was that SCK itself should change so as to embrace such cells. At the same time there was a new openness to talking, studying and praying with Christians of other denominations in order to make friendships and to understand one another better.

Is it good enough to say to interested non-Anglicans: 'Sorry you can't join us, but if you want to borrow our techniques, you are welcome' and carry on as before? We can do this, but if we do, we must face the fact that SCK will never make any contribution to the service of Christ in social, ecumenical, educational or industrial fields and we must be very clear why we are making this choice.

The alternative is a Christian cell movement which transcends all denominations. A movement which will contain, as at present, Anglican companies with a concern for the spiritual life of Anglican parishes – but also Roman Catholic, Quaker, Congregationalist, Methodist companies with a concern for their own churches – *plus* – for those who felt called to join them – mixed groups concerned with social problems or a deeper understanding of their own faith. (Norman, SCK Newsletter, 1964)

In 1964, SCK celebrated its twenty-first birthday with a week-long conference held at Swanwick from 28 August to 4 September with an attendance estimated at two hundred (Norman, Servants of Christ the King: Companies to be Open to All Christians, 1964). On the Sunday, the whole conference was transported to Coventry Cathedral for a coming-of-age service. The address was given by Stephen Verney, Canon

Missioner of the Coventry diocese and a member of the Central Company of SCK. Stephen Verney had come to the Coventry diocese as Diocesan Missioner in 1958, when the new cathedral was still under construction. He described his work in a book, *Fire in Coventry*, published in 1964 and rediscovered and re-published in 2010 with an enthusiastic introduction by the current Bishop of Coventry (Verney, 2010). After taking up his post, Stephen Verney began by meeting with clergy in small groups, talking little but listening carefully and trying to hear the answer to the question 'What is the Spirit saying to the churches?'. Out of one of these meetings came a group of clergy in neighbouring parishes who together became convinced that what was needed was not only a newly consecrated cathedral but a consecrated people living round it. The group brought a diverse collection of clergy together in a fellowship which they had not experienced before. Other clergy groups began to form. This was described by Stephen Verney as the 'first ripple'. It was to be followed by the gathering in of the laity in three ever widening circles, beginning with small clergy-laity groups, continuing with a wide range of meetings and activities in parishes, and culminating in a gathering up of the whole diocese in mission and consecration in 1962. None of these activities bore the name of SCK, though Stephen Verney's book does record a meeting in a church hall addressed by Olive Parker and Richard Babington (Verney, 2010, pp. 83-4). But the whole approach to mission based on small groups, listening for God's will for the here and now, and obedient to the call, is thoroughly consistent with that of SCK and reminiscent of Richard Babington's evangelisation work a decade earlier in Ipswich as described in chapter eight of *An Adventure in Discipleship* (Lloyd, An Adventure in Discipleship, 1953, pp. 107-119).

On the following day the Swanwick conference returned to business with a talk from Olive Parker. Her tone was not optimistic.

> SCK in 1964 is not only exceedingly small but frail in health. There are, I would consider, fewer than 100 really active companies, with a few more hanging on with very small numbers, hoping that better days will come again. SCK is largely female in composition; and its average age is high. A few young people have been in touch with the movement from time to time, but they have not in most cases succeeded in becoming members of companies. (Parker, Call to Commitment, 1964, p. 5)

According to Olive Parker, the weakness of SCK lay not only in numbers and demographics, but in the lack, or perhaps loss, of vision of SCK as a way of life.

If pushed, most companies would talk of the value of prayer together and how important their fellowship is to them. They would point out what busy people all their members are. They often give the impression that SCK is a receptacle for the odd jobs and a pleasant occasion spiritually. There appears to be little sense that here is the main-spring of all their activity and the home base from which the members go out into their lives in the church and the world.

One does meet this latter attitude occasionally and nearly always in new companies. They have still the light of vision in their eyes which are often fresh from reading *An Adventure in Discipleship*. While one rejoices to see the miracle happening again, one has a sadness and anxiety at the back of one's mind. What will their company be like in three, five, seven years? Will they be desperately trying to keep it going? Will they be keeping to a period of silence as their main reason for meeting, while still unsure as to what waiting on God really means? Will they be less and less able to find purpose in their company life, using their time together to hold a controlled discussion which is uncontrolled by any sense of urgency or purpose, but given over to the reiteration of pious platitudes? Will they, in short, have followed what is too often the pattern in SCK, of a company becoming a diffuse and vaguely organised prayer group, with its fellowship little more demanding than the friendship found in any group of people meeting regularly? (Parker, Call to Commitment, 1964, pp. 5-6)

Olive Parker went on to reflect on the causes of what she saw as the decline of SCK: the reluctance to proclaim SCK as a way of life; resistance to any form of organisation; reluctance to tackle anything too definite because 'we exist to pray and ... our prayer means passing from the definite to the indefinite'; and resistance to training because 'training implies direction from another person or persons and so must be rejected because we are under the immediate guidance of the Holy Spirit'. Against this, she pointed out the need for study of the scriptures if corporate spiritual life was not to become attenuated and idiosyncratic. Companies ought also to be aware of current thinking on group relationships; to be able to identify local problems and existing resources; and to learn 'attitudes of acceptance and skills of caring which are a necessity in the training of the most agnostic social worker' (Parker, Call to Commitment, 1964, p. 8). From training would spring knowledge of the truth and right attitudes.

The conference responded to these concerns, asserting in a unanimously agreed policy statement that God's call to SCK was still clear and definite: it was to combat fear, insecurity and apathy in the world by loving God and each other, by waiting on him always, by asking that our wills should be conformed to his will, by loving our fellow men in all situations, accepting them for what they are and offering ourselves in their service.

> Let there be no mistake that this is demanding and costly and that the bonds of love can cut as well as bind. For the world is corrupt and we are called to join in Christ's redemptive work. It is urgent that our commitment to him should be deepened so that we can fulfil our vocation, and to do that the Servants of Christ the King must be articulate and disciplined, compassionate and informed. (SCK Central Company, 1964)

To this end, the conference supported the development of training schemes and a regional organisation to be responsible for deepening the life of companies, promoting new companies and launching experiments. It affirmed that 'the commitment of a company is not only to its own rule of life, but to representing the movement as a whole in the place where it exists', adding that this commitment included trying to form new companies and contributing financially to the movement. Finally,

> The work of the movement in relation to the needs of the world cannot be accomplished solely by Anglicans; in future companies consisting of committed Christians of all kinds will be recognised. (SCK Central Company, 1964)

As a corollary to this, though not included in the policy statement, the requirement that each company should have a priest-adviser was modified and became only a recommendation. Companies working within a congregation were duty bound to secure the goodwill of the parish priest or minister. However, this left open the possibility of companies drawing members from several different congregations and denominations, requiring no clergy guidance or consent at all.

Thus the doors were opened to non-Anglicans. In fact, some interdenominational groups had already been meeting, including one in Devon reported in the SCK Newsletter in February 1964. Despite the conference decision, which was referred to at the time as 'going ecumenical', SCK remained preponderantly Anglican. The first appointment of a non-Anglican non-clerical Warden came in 1996, and even then only after a long list of Anglican clergy had received and declined invitations to consider the post. An earlier Warden who left the

Church of England for another denomination had felt it necessary to resign his office in SCK (Church Times, 1988). Right to the end in 2014, the daily Eucharist at the annual conference continued to be an Anglican celebration. Some non-Anglicans present (including two Wardens) did not feel free to receive the sacrament, a matter of sadness for themselves and the conference as a whole. The majority of members of most if not all companies were Anglicans, and even among those belonging to other churches a good many had been Anglicans at some time during their lives or were familiar with Anglican ways. But the inclusion of non-Anglicans had significant results, since it loosened the ties between SCK companies and Anglican parishes. There was no upsurge of new companies within other denominations – the existence of a Methodist company for example, or a Roman Catholic company, might have set a new pattern – but this was not to be.

The development of training schemes called for by the conference went ahead with two publications in 1965: *Training Course on Being Informed* ('suggestions for Bible study and group discussion on the practical results of belief in the Trinity'); and *Training Course on Being Articulate* ('discussion on ways of presenting SCK to others'). By this time SCK was even selling a training folder, perhaps with the implication that more training publications were expected, though no further such publications exist in the SCK archives.

Roger Lloyd died suddenly and unexpectedly in September 1966, at the age of 65. After he handed over the wardenship of SCK in 1961 he had remained in the background but still came to SCK conferences. He remained a member of the Executive Company though unable to attend their meetings. There was much more to Roger Lloyd than SCK: he had many gifts and these were used to the full as Sub-Dean of Winchester and passionate advocate of cathedrals, spiritual director, railway enthusiast, historian and, above all, writer. He had at least thirty books published as well as hundreds of newspaper articles, many of them in *The Guardian*, *Church Times*, *The Spectator* and *Time and Tide*. His last book ('the big book' as he called it) was a history of the Church of England in the twentieth century (Lloyd, The Church of England 1900-1965, 1966), a complete revision and rethinking of two earlier volumes published in 1946 and 1950 respectively. But SCK was close to his heart. In his last letter to Olive Parker, written only a day or two before his death, he accepted the title of honorary adviser to the Executive Company, but added 'In fact, as I think I wrote to you, I think of myself now as Prophet-in-Ordinary to the movement. And so I will be, as and when it may be wanted.' He was a prophet, but also an enabler. As Olive Parker wrote:

He rejoiced in the achievements and talents of the other, helping to bring out ideas and to inspire action. When I had talked with him, I always felt immensely energetic and purposeful. If I had gone to see him bewildered and frustrated, I came away with renewed faith in what we are about and eager to work out the next step. Yet it was difficult to remember anything he had said, but I sensed that my best ideas were from him to be worked out by me. (Parker, SCK Newsletter, 1966, pp. 3-7)

Roger Lloyd was a leader who could lead from beside, recognising and nurturing the inspiration of others. To quote the words on his monument in Winchester Cathedral, 'He loved much'. With his death SCK lost its first prophet. The times were already difficult for SCK and for the church. Another prophetic voice was desperately needed, but for this SCK had to wait.

CHAPTER FOUR

WAITING FOR GONVILLE

Gonville Aubie ffrench-Beytagh was born in Shanghai in 1912 and educated in England. After spending a rather wild youth in New Zealand, he moved to South Africa in the 1930s. It was there that he found Christ and felt a call to the priesthood. From 1939 he served as priest and Diocesan Missioner in the Johannesburg diocese. He was appointed Dean of Salisbury, Rhodesia (now Harare, Zimbabwe) in 1955. A parishioner there gave him a copy of Roger Lloyd's *An Adventure in Discipleship* and he was enthused by it. While on leave in England he made a point of meeting Olive Parker and taking part in an SCK company meeting. He went back to Rhodesia and in 1958 started an SCK company consisting of members of the Salisbury Cathedral congregation. The company found a common concern in creating opportunities for African and European Anglicans to meet socially on equal terms. One of the members of the company was Alison Norman, who was then in Salisbury working on a local newspaper. She and many others encountered in Gonville a living faith. Some of them returned to England (Alison Norman in 1959, others later), bringing with them the experience of an SCK company whose waiting on God had led them to accept risks and to take on pioneering work. Gonville ffrench-Beytagh was an invited speaker at the 1963 SCK conference. He was appointed Dean of Johannesburg in 1965. The world was soon to hear much more of him.

Meanwhile, SCK in England was losing energy. Richard Babington had taken over from Roger Lloyd as Warden of SCK in 1961. Within less than a year of Roger Lloyd's death he was already warning SCK of his approaching retirement. Although he agreed to continue as Warden of SCK for the time being, he was also preparing to retire from his posts as

Archdeacon of Exeter and Canon Residentiary of Exeter Cathedral. Both retirements eventually took place in 1970.

Another key person was also preparing to withdraw from the central position which she had held in the movement. Olive Parker retired as Secretary in 1967. She was a clear-minded administrator who helped SCK to think about its structures and not to put such thinking aside as somehow 'unspiritual':

> I do not consider either organisation or efficiency as suspect; we have a calling to root organisation in prayer and to show efficiency with love. (Parker, An Essay in Self-Examination, 1963, p. 7)

But Olive Parker's gifts to SCK were not just in administration. For a time she was effectively the voice of SCK, travelling around England to spread the message, editing the Newsletter and acting as the first point of contact for enquirers who had read her book or one of the leaflets which SCK was now putting out. In 1972 she and her husband Jack left London to live on the Isle of Skye. There she continued to live an active life, throwing herself into working for the local community with the same energy and clarity of vision which she had brought to SCK. She died in 1990, having served as a district councillor and chairman of the housing committee, church secretary and promoter of the arts on the Isle of Skye.

After the retirement of Richard Babington, SCK had no Warden for the time being. A new Secretary, Jim Brierley, had been appointed to succeed Olive Parker, but the tasks involved in keeping the movement together were now shared more widely than they had been before. For example, the SCK Newsletter had from the beginning been edited by the Warden or the Secretary, with the exception of only one edition. The Huddersfield SCK company had undertaken the editorship in April 1952, but for whatever reason this had not continued. Roger Lloyd himself wrote most of the articles in the Newsletter during his wardenship, after which articles by a wider range of writers were published under the editorship of Olive Parker. Only in 1969 was the editorship of the Newsletter taken on by Peter Broxis.

The rapid decline in church membership in Britain which had begun in the early sixties continued, with decreasing numbers of baptisms and confirmations, fewer vocations to the priesthood, and closure or merger of many theological colleges. The statistics of the time do not appear to show a corresponding decline in belief in God, or at any rate in some kind of divine influence on the world. The best-selling book *The Secular City* by Harvey Cox (1965), disturbing for some and energising for others, called for Christians to leave the religious ghetto which Harvey Cox claimed the churches had become, and to recognise that God is just as present in the so-called 'secular' as in the 'religious' realms of life. Others rejected the churches altogether but held on to a personal spirituality: a condition sometimes labelled as 'believing without belonging'.

What did this mean for SCK? On the one hand, the founders of SCK had never supported the rigid division between the religious and the secular, and had always asserted that God was present and at work in the secular world. They had started a movement, a fellowship of fellowships of lay people living in the secular world, which was to help the church to move out of the ghetto into which it seemed to have been confined. On the other hand, these lay fellowships remained closely bound to the church and particularly to the parish system of the Church of England, even though the movement was now officially open to other denominations. SCK had found it difficult to make any impression on that part of the secular world which it was originally designed to enter, namely the world of work. Moreover, the whole idea of SCK was based on belonging, most intensely within the small local group or 'company', but at the same time in the wider concentric circles of the local church community and the organised church and churches as a whole. The SCK practice of waiting on God promoted a certain freedom and did not in itself impose uniformity of belief, but it was set within a commitment to fellowship and was meant to lead to unity in corporate discernment. Although it had long ago decided that it was not to be an Order it made big demands and some members still regarded its rule and promise as quasi-monastic, though adapted to the world of the lay person. This was a time when monastic vocations in Britain had fallen to a new low and some Anglican orders such as the Society of the Sacred Mission were entering a crisis (Mason, 1993, pp. 246-68).

With the Secretary of SCK gone and its Warden ready to go, with declining membership in the churches, and with the apparently widespread desire for some kind of change, it is not surprising that a feeling of lostness grew within SCK. Alison Norman wrote about an open meeting held in March 1969 to discuss the programme for the coming annual conference:

> Somehow the movement felt inert, without a sense of energy and purpose or direction. We were worried about the conference because it was so expensive and we doubted whether people saw any real point in coming. 'What, after all, is the point?' we asked ourselves. Someone remarked that 'something died at last year's conference' and concluded that this year we had got to begin by really facing the

implications of what happened then. ... It became clear that the conference was going to have to think seriously whether SCK should go on in its present form. We needed to ask how much it would really matter if the organisational trappings of SCK packed up, leaving its basic ideas to propagate themselves and the existing companies to carry on as they wished. ... Had the sense of the power of the Spirit gone out of the movement just because we were using it as a defence against change and a way of clinging to the safe and familiar when it should be just the opposite? What really was it that SCK had lost? (Norman, Impressions of the Open Meeting, 1969)

The meeting went on from thoughts of death to hope for new life. Might SCK, born in a very different time, be given a new call to service to a world of 'all things new'? The planning of the conference went ahead. Alison Norman continued:

I think it is just possible that that moment will prove to have been the beginning of a new life for SCK, though perhaps in some radically-changed and almost unrecognisable form. (Norman, Impressions of the Open Meeting, 1969)

The theme of the conference was to be 'Resurrection'. A large part of its purpose would be to explore a possible relationship between SCK and an Anglican renewal group, Parish and People. This group, founded in 1949, had been largely responsible for popularising the parish communion as the main worship event in Anglican parishes. It was now heavily involved in the process of setting up an Ecumenical Renewal Group (soon to become 'ONE for Christian Renewal') in order 'to seek to promote the renewal of Christ's church for its mission in the world'. Members of the group were meant to 'express their Christian faith in political and social affairs [and to] work for new life and reform in the Church and organic unity between its parts'. Parish and People was prepared to give up its own separate existence and put its full resources at the disposal of the new ecumenical body once it was fully in existence. (In the event this never came about: Parish and People went on as a campaigning voice within the Church of England until 2013.) The interest of some SCK people in Parish and People was twofold: as a potential home and as an example.

Are we failing to let people know that we have aspirations to being an ecumenical renewal group? Or is progress always through death and are we being asked to follow the example of Parish and People? (SCK Central Company, 1969, p. 12)

As it turned out, anxieties about the conference were fully justified. It had to be called off because of insufficient numbers. Instead, a one-day autumn conference was held in London in November. The theme was still 'Resurrection'. John Hammersley, executive secretary of Parish and People, was the main speaker and there were papers on ecumenical renewal and the questions about the future of SCK raised by the open meeting in March. In addition there was a paper by the Secretary, Jim Brierley, questioning the name 'Servants of Christ the King'.

> Our title 'The Servants of Christ the King' has been criticised on more than one occasion in the past, and the recent outbreak of a fresh crop of objections might not have called for comment, had they not been made at a time when the future of SCK is being reconsidered. If we are not to lose ourselves in a new organisation such as that born out of Parish & People and other renewal groups ... the question of a new name does not arise. But if we are to be reborn as a separate movement, we may need a new name. ... Critics often complain that our title gives SCK an air of religiosity which is off putting to newcomers, who are not to know that, if anything, we are the reverse. Others say that it suggests a high church background. ... Another common objection is that it abrogates to a small group a title which rightly belongs to all Christians. Young people seem to feel these objections particularly strongly, and there are reasons to believe that our failure to attract new young members may be due, in part, to distaste for our name. ... [A correspondent] says that the name suggests a barrier as between servant and king – 'artificial, false and I would not consider pleasing to Christ'. He feels that the word 'king' is superfluous and postulates an attitude right out of date. (Brierley, 1969)

Doubts and hesitations continued. A member of the Central Company, asked to contribute thoughts for the future of the movement in 1970, exclaimed that 'what is needed is a prophet for SCK'. Another wrote, after attending the 1971 conference, that the movement 'had all the symptoms of a dying animal'. SCK had not given up its life to make way for a wider-based movement, but neither had it managed to attract more than a few non-Anglicans into its companies. Some members hoped that SCK, committed as it was to attending to the Holy Spirit, would discover an affinity with the charismatic movement which was beginning to stir in Anglicanism as in other denominations. The 1971 conference was addressed on this subject by Brother Jeremy CR. Some members recorded experiencing 'baptism in the Spirit' at one of the services towards the end of the conference. But others did not have this experience and SCK as a movement did not take this direction. (Carder, 1973)

The prophet awaited by SCK was at last on the way. Gonville ffrench-Beytagh had been tried and sentenced in South Africa in 1970 for political offences and held in solitary confinement (ffrench-Beytagh, *Encountering Darkness*, 1973). Gonville's conviction and sentence were overturned on appeal in 1972. In August of the same year Gonville attended the SCK conference where he gave a talk about his experiences in jail. He spoke about how he had tried to pray and had been granted an awareness of Our Lord's presence as real as in the Eucharist. A session which had been intended as a social half-hour between the Central Company and Gonville ffrench-Beytagh became a depressing examination of the state of the movement. These thoughts were put to the whole conference on the following day, after which Gonville spoke about the steps he would take, if it were left to him, 'to recall the movement to itself'. At that moment, Gonville was made for SCK and SCK was made for Gonville. He was adopted as Warden with acclamation. He described what happened next in a letter which he sent to all SCK companies:

> It all started with me being rather rude to the conference as a whole. I had listened to the company reports as they were given and I felt that if this was SCK (which I was pretty sure it wasn't, because I believe the companies under-rated themselves on what they were doing) – that if this was it, then I wanted no part nor lot with it. I realised that deep friendships had been formed in SCK but much of the early impact of the movement seemed to me to have been lost. There appeared to be intercession groups and bible study groups, but you do not have to belong to SCK to do these two very necessary things.
>
> The essence of SCK seems to me to be contained in Roger Lloyd's book *Adventure in Discipleship* which I think is a good sub-title for SCK, but where was the 'adventure' in all that I heard, and where the 'discipleship'? Because discipleship of course is simply discipline – the words mean almost the same thing. It seemed to me that we needed more clear cut discipleship and discipline and certainly a strong sense of adventure.
>
> It also seemed to me that the heart of both discipleship and adventure lay in the essential SCK activity of 'waiting on God'. (ffrench-Beytagh, Letter to all Companies, 1972)

Such a recall to basics was not unprecedented in the life of SCK. Expectancy and total self-offering in waiting on God were high intentions which some groups never realised in practice and which could easily decay even when they were there at the beginning. However, Gonville was not only concerned to bring SCK back to the original vision. He had a new sense of SCK's calling.

> [T]he organised structured church as we know it may have to go through a process akin to death and its new shape may well take the form of small companies of committed Christians such as the companies of the Servants of Christ the King. I believe that we are in the forefront of great changes in the church. Therefore a very great responsibility lies on us, the Servants of Christ the King, to be open and aware to where we may be led so that we may take our place in helping to lead the church into its new life.
>
> There is a growing interest, especially among young people, in the life of the Spirit taking many shapes or forms – in Pentecostalism and other forms of Christian community – in Eastern mysticism – in ecumenism and indeed in anything which manifests love. In our companies led by the Spirit we have a 'mystique' which can take its place and make its special contribution to all of this. In addition, we have the power to turn it into action, into service and into the application of love in practice. All of this is what I believe we are called to be and do. (ffrench-Beytagh, Letter to all Companies, 1972)

Gonville ffrench-Beytagh was aware of the difficulties, physical, cultural and practical as well as spiritual, which could be encountered in waiting on God in the SCK manner. Together with his introductory letter, quoted above, he sent a paper entitled 'Advice on Waiting upon God' (ffrench-Beytagh, Advice on Waiting upon God, 1972). This was later to become an SCK booklet which, with some editing and updating, remained in print throughout the rest of the life of SCK. The original version is reproduced as Document C in Part III of this volume.

Gonville brought new hope to SCK. He was a much-sought spiritual director who had suffered and continued to suffer for his faith. His name was well known in and far beyond church circles. His life exemplified the close relationship between prayer and action to which SCK aspired. He was passionate in his love of Christ and open to the movings of 'the Lord, the Holy Spirit'. He taught and encouraged total openness to the Spirit and was not afraid to recommend techniques learned from Eastern spirituality as well as endorsing the charismatic renewal movement. His books and booklets, realised and published with the help of Alison Norman and other SCK members, were valuable and widely praised. (ffrench-Beytagh, Encountering Darkness, 1973) (ffrench-Beytagh & Norman, Encountering Light, 1975) (ffrench-Beytagh, Facing

Depression, 1978) (ffrench-Beytagh & Hodges, A Glimpse of Glory, 1986) (ffrench-Beytagh & Hodges, Tree of Glory, 1988) (ffrench-Beytagh & Robinson, Out of the Depths: Encountering Depression, 2010)

Yet although Gonville ffrench-Beytagh had a profound influence on those who knew him, deep unease in SCK continued. Perhaps part of the problem was that SCK had set such high standards. Gonville's recall to those standards may even have increased the anxiety which was already there. Alison Norman found this anxiety when she went around the country visiting SCK companies in November 1973.

> [T]here were some things which I met everywhere – the almost overwhelming sense of warmth and welcome and belonging with which I was met, the way people talked about the depth of their relationships in SCK and how much this meant to them and a general feeling of falling short of what people felt they should be being and doing. 'I suppose we're not "proper" SCK' was said over and over again. (Norman, Pilgrim's report, 1974, pp. 21-2)

Although the demands of SCK were more severe than those of the newer Christian meditation groups, they became less institutionalised. From 1964 onwards there were several attempts to strengthen the SCK rule and promise and to adapt them to cross-denominational membership (SCK Central Company Paper, c. 1972), but despite this they began to fall into disuse. Gonville ffrench-Beytagh had acquired in childhood an absolutist attitude to promise-keeping which had led to a strong reluctance for promise-making. He tried to hold SCK members to what he saw as the essence of SCK, but he did this by exhortation and inspiration and not by appeal to a rule. The gradual disappearance of a corporate rule, although in keeping with the times, might even have increased the anxiety of some members who felt that they were somehow not quite living up to 'proper' SCK standards but could not put their finger on what they were missing.

Gonville ffrench-Beytagh several times expressed the desire that SCK would 'grow by proliferation'. By this he appears to have meant that members of SCK would plant new companies wherever they went. He was disappointed in this hope (SCK Central Company, 1979). There were a few notable exceptions, though even some of these required considerable prodding from Gonville before they got down to arranging for him to come and address meetings in their new parishes. SCK in the 1940s and early 1950s had been a largely youthful movement. Those who had stayed since those days were now its backbone. When they moved home, it was often to retire or to look after aged parents. Settling into a new home, a new parish and a new stage of life may have left little energy for proliferating SCK.

At the same time a new generation was discovering Christian meditation. Although other groups such as the Fellowship of Contemplative Prayer (FCP) had been in existence since the 1940s, the Julian Meetings started as an ecumenical initiative in 1973 and quickly grew. Contemplative silence was part of the SCK tradition too but SCK demanded more and its practice of waiting on God had a more complex structure which some may have found constraining. There was no conflict between the two approaches and some SCK members managed to remain involved in both. For example in 1981 Peter Thorburn, later to become Warden of SCK, organised a meeting in Manchester at which Gonville ffrench-Beytagh addressed a meeting of many Christian traditions with a practice of silence including Benedictines and Quakers as well as FCP and SCK.

Gonville ffrench-Beytagh retired as Warden of SCK in 1984. He was a passionate lover of Christ who was able to articulate what his Christian faith meant to him. His inner life fed his contributions to the world and gave him courage for his work in South Africa. He brought a spirituality that enthused like-minded people and left its mark on SCK. No one could fill the space which he vacated when he ceased to be Warden. It was time for change, but many faithful members of SCK were to see themselves as 'Gonville's people' for years to come.

CHAPTER FIVE

STILL WAITING

Gonville ffrench-Beytagh was succeeded as Warden by Robin Bennett, an Anglican priest who had served in several parishes in the East End of London and was then Adult Education Officer at the Church of England General Synod Board of Education. He was about to take up a new post in the Worcester diocese where, with the title of Archdeacon of Dudley, he would be responsible for adult education.

Robin Bennett had grown up in Ipswich with SCK all around him, though he was not aware of it at the time. His vicar was a member of the Ipswich clergy company which Richard Babington had started. Members of this clergy company had seen the planting of lay companies as part of their concern, and by 1953 ten parish companies had come into being in the Ipswich area (Lloyd, An Adventure in Discipleship, 1953, pp. 108-9, 112). Robin Bennett was to come into contact with SCK again several more times after that, but it was while serving as Adult Education Officer at Church House Westminster that he began to read the SCK literature which came into the office. He became convinced that this was something important which he should follow up. He met with the Central Company and was invited to speak at an SCK conference.

By this time Gonville ffrench-Beytagh had already served more than ten years as Warden and was urging SCK to appoint a successor. It was hoped that Robin Bennett's many contacts would help to bring younger people into SCK. He had an impressive record as an agent of change, was good at listening to and enabling people. The 1984 conference appointed Robin Bennett as the new Warden. The retiring Warden was careful to ensure that the handover was complete and did not intervene in SCK affairs between his retirement and his death in 1991.

It cannot have been easy to succeed Gonville. But Robin Bennett brought different gifts and received much love and acceptance. He understood the need for good organisation and drew attention to it in a way which had not been seen since the days of Olive Parker. He confronted the doubts which were again being expressed about whether SCK was still doing its job, or had a job to do, labelling these 'the SCK deathwish' and reassuring doubters that the Lord would make it clear when SCK really had to come to an end.

It was only later that SCK members became aware that Robin Bennett was going through a time of change and was at a difficult point in his career. He resigned as Archdeacon of Dudley in 1986, then resigned altogether from Anglican holy orders and joined the Quakers in 1987. At the 1988 SCK conference he announced his resignation as Warden. The *Church Times* reported him as saying that he believed that SCK was accustomed to a style of leadership which, from his new Quaker perspective, he no longer felt capable of giving (Church Times, 1988). Robin Bennett had been, though for a short while and unplanned, the first non-Anglican non-ordained Warden of SCK. Attempts were made to persuade him to stay on, but he was clear that he had to leave though maintaining his links with SCK and continuing to support the movement.

After an interregnum Peter Thorburn was appointed as Warden in 1989. His long experience and involvement in SCK made him an obvious choice. In retrospect members asked themselves why they had not thought of him sooner. Their eyes were opened at the annual conference, where he gave the opening talk and took a leading role in running the conference. As Alison Norman wrote:

> [W]e saw not a new but a different Peter, whose light had been deliberately dimmed so as not to compete with the 'official' leaders, and the way he celebrated the Eucharist took us back to Gonville. (Norman, A New Warden, 1989)

Peter Thorburn undertook to serve as Warden for five years. He was in retirement after a ministry which had included hospital chaplaincy as well as parish duties in London and the North of England and (briefly) in the United States. He had a deep concern for health and healing and in the last twenty years of his ministry had been a hospital chaplain in Manchester. Peter Thorburn had first become aware of SCK when he read Roger Lloyd's book *An Adventure in Discipleship*. This led him to start an SCK company in Wigan in Lancashire, where he was at that time Vicar of the church of St Michael and All Angels. He was already a member of the Fellowship of Contemplative Prayer (FCP) and continued in that membership as well as in SCK. He was a bridge between people who practised various methods of silence.

Peter Thorburn and his brother Austin, also an Anglican priest, took every opportunity to make SCK more widely known. The *Church Times* could no longer be relied on to carry news of SCK, as it had in the 1960s and up to the mid-1970s. Austin was energetic in the function of Enquiries Correspondent, ensuring that SCK was listed in Christian directories and other publications, writing articles for the church press, bringing SCK to the attention of other movements in which he was also a member, meticulously answering the enquiries which came in, and keeping in touch with past enquirers. Peter wrote a new leaflet in which he managed to distil the essence of SCK into five hundred words. In this leaflet, apparently for the first time, some emphasis was placed on the ecumenical dimension of SCK.

> The first [SCK] companies ... were formed in Church of England parishes with the Vicar as adviser. But it was right, and inevitable, that after some years SCK should grow into an ecumenical instrument, and be available to Christians of any tradition and in any continent of the world. It was the most natural discovery that silence, which is essential for 'waiting upon God', should be able to bring together pilgrims hitherto separated by the weight of their differing historical, doctrinal, and liturgical traditions. In this way SCK began to learn, from the Society of Friends on the one hand, and from the contemplative religious orders on the other, something of the crucial link between prayer and action. 'They also serve who only stand and wait' was written about the ministry of the holy angels, whose mission to God's world is made possible by their unflinching attention to the face of God. Like the angels, SCK tries to seek God's face and to listen to his word in order to be of service to God's world. (Peter Thorburn, 1990)

Peter Thorburn came to the end of his five years as Warden of SCK in 1994 but continued to be active in the movement. From 1993 onwards, Central Company sounded out a long series of Anglican clerics who had some past connection with SCK, most of them recently retired, but none was willing to take on the office of Warden. In 1994, the SCK conference met a candidate recommended by the previous Warden as his successor but was unable to make an appointment. After waiting on God, the conference recorded that 'it was felt a disadvantage that he had never belonged to an SCK company, and members would have liked to have known him better before making a decision' (SCK Conference, 1994). Further names were suggested, but finally a decision was made to widen the search, and by implication to drop the requirement for prior experience of SCK. Some members had been pressing for this all along, feeling that SCK needed to open itself to fresh inspiration. Letters were sent to leaders of mainstream churches, asking if they could suggest people who might be approached to accept the office of Warden.

> Previous Wardens have all been priests of the Anglican church, but now the movement is asking whether it is reasonable that the Warden should yet again be a white, male, ordained Anglican. Perhaps SCK service to the church could best be led by someone with a vocation of well-publicised social concern and an established network of active contacts? (Austin Thorburn, Draft letter to church leaders, 1994)

The only positive reply to this letter came from Britain Yearly Meeting of the Religious Society of Friends (Quakers), putting forward my name. The group who had been given the task of searching for and appointing a Warden (grandly titled 'Stewards of the Interregnum') took up this suggestion and wrote to me. After several meetings and visits to SCK companies, I agreed to serve as Warden for a period of three years. I was an experienced Quaker clerk and elder and found much that was familiar in the SCK way of waiting on God.

The decision to appoint me was perhaps not quite as radical a change as some expected at the time. I was white and male and though not an ordained Anglican had come to Quakerism from a thoroughly Anglican background. I had never quite given up my links with the Anglican church and had renewed them in the years immediately preceding my appointment. My training in spiritual direction and retreat leading had been on courses run by Anglicans. I was comfortable with Anglican ways. My kind of Anglicanism was twenty-five years out of date, but this might rather have suited many SCK members.

I undertook to travel round England visiting members and companies, to try to gain some understanding of the state and future prospects of the movement, and to report back to the next conference. I found great faithfulness to 'the SCK way' but also much self-doubt and self-deprecation. I put forward three possible versions of the future for prayerful consideration:

1. continuing in slow decline;

2. releasing energies by laying down formal structures;

3. finding new life through reinterpreting the vision. (Bridge, Reflections on the Future of SCK, 1997)

The last of these was the hardest to accept and the hardest to envisage.

> New life is different from what we have known before ... We cannot claim it for SCK, for we cannot direct God's purposes. If it is given to us, the way to it may look to us like death. (Bridge, Reflections on the Future of SCK, 1997)

Although I was not aware of it at the time, much of this echoed the discussion which had gone on around the 'Resurrection' theme back in 1969. What was perhaps new was my attempt to define a set of five SCK 'essentials'. The intended implication was that SCK stood for something important, but that everything non-essential in SCK – organisation, practice, language, name and even identity – was non-essential and could be discarded if it stood in the way of sharing with others.

> As a starting-point for our exercise together, I suggest that there are five essentials of the SCK vision:
>
> 1.   Christian basis;
>
> 2.   belief in the working of the Holy Spirit in the group;
>
> 3.   contemplative prayer;
>
> 4.   listening to and respecting every member of the group;
>
> 5.   commitment to acting together.
>
> If we are clear about the essentials, we can become free to let go of all else, including aspects of our current practice and even if necessary our identity as SCK. (Bridge, Reflections on the Future of SCK, 1997)

The May 1997 conference considered the report. It endorsed my five essentials, but did not take on the implication that all else was inessential and might have to be dispensed with. Instead, the conference affirmed:

> We believe that this movement has a special calling and is still needed by the church and the world today, as well as by our own circle of people who have been associated with SCK in the past. We want the movement to continue, both in local groups and in appropriate central structures. We recognise that the movement has a loving responsibility to all those who have served in and through it in the past, and we will keep this in mind when considering our future central structures. We wish to keep the name 'Servants of Christ the King'. (SCK Conference, 1997)

The loving responsibility of the movement to its members – many of them by now elderly, scattered and unable to take part in a local company – was an increasing concern for SCK as a whole. A 'Shadow Company' had been in existence since 1965, consisting of members who had no local company but undertook to 'shadow' a specific SCK leader in prayer. The Shadow Company had around thirty members at this time, bound together by a newsletter as well as by individual shadowing relationships. However, there was a growing number of scattered members who did not feel a vocation to this kind of shadowing relationship or were simply unable to undertake it. The Central Company had already recognised this earlier in the year when it appointed a Pastoral Correspondent (SCK, 1997).

Halfway through my term of office as Warden, I transferred my denominational allegiance from Quakers to the Russian Orthodox Church. This seems to have caused hardly a ripple. The only significant change for SCK was that I was no longer able to receive the Anglican sacraments at SCK conferences, whereas before as a Quaker-Anglican I had felt no problem in doing so. Although there was some sadness on both sides, most people understood or at least tolerated the situation. There were precedents: SCK already had a few Roman Catholic and Orthodox members who faced the same difficulty when they came to conferences.

The 1997 conference had decided that SCK should carry on much as before with only a few administrative changes. After this there was little appetite for radical re-examination. With prayer and discussion the movement had come to the conclusion that its work was not yet done, and that there was still time for new opportunities to open. A good deal of effort continued to go into writing and distributing leaflets, getting articles into church newspapers, placing entries in directories and setting up a website. A trickle of enquiries came in, many of them asking to be referred to a local company, but the declining number and limited geographical distribution of companies often made this difficult or impossible. Enquirers were encouraged to find colleagues and start their own companies, but this rarely if ever happened in practice.

I had undertaken to serve as Warden for three years. The hunt for a successor began in good time with the appointment of a search group. In waiting on God together the search group came to the conclusion that they should give up compiling candidate lists of well-known people and instead should ask a religious community to nominate one of its members. The group wrote to the Community of Saint Mary the Virgin at Wantage. Mother Barbara Claire CSMV responded agreeing to a meeting at the convent. As a result of this it was not long before SCK received and gratefully endorsed the nomination of Sister Anne Julian CSMV as its next

Warden. Although Sister Anne Julian had not previously been a member of an SCK company, she had long been aware of the movement and had directed people to it.

Sister Anne Julian was the first woman and the first religious to serve as Warden. Her appointment was a reaffirmation of the SCK principle of being before doing and reflected a desire for deeper spiritual grounding. Some of this had perhaps been missed during the preceding lay wardenship. Sister Anne Julian made it clear that she would be ready to preside at SCK conferences and attend Central Company meetings but could not otherwise commit herself to travel round the country or attach herself to a local company. Instead she provided a calm point of reference. The whole community of Wantage sisters upheld SCK in prayer. SCK had long ago decided that it was not to be an Order, but its roots lay in a sense of vocation and commitment to Christ and community which had much in common with religious orders. Anne Julian recognised this in the SCK way of waiting on God.

> In reality, we are all of us one heart-beat away from death! To me it seems that this is precisely why SCK with its 'method' and customs is right in the forefront, always having an attitude of mind which seeks the will of God in whatever comes, responding to that call in some sense with our fellow-servants, and so preparing for the time when God will call each of us home to himself and his welcome. Well done, good and faithful servant. (Sister Anne Julian CSMV, 2007)

For Anne Julian the 'attitude of mind which seeks the will of God in whatever comes' was what really mattered in SCK. It was to this rather than the specifics of the SCK method that she continued to draw attention. She was able to place SCK's way of waiting on God within a wider context of ways of discernment. She could be gently critical when she felt that some groups were relying on a too narrow understanding of the method, or were turning what was meant to be a corporate seeking of God's will into an interesting discussion.

After eight years of wardenship, Anne Julian's health, which had several times given cause for concern, took another turn for the worse. She gave notice that she would not be long able to continue:

> In my own personal waiting on God, it has been made abundantly clear to me that I must relinquish my wardenship of SCK. I shall be 82 in August this year and I am becoming increasingly infirm, wearing out all over and becoming dottier by the day! ... I do very little as Warden and it may be that you will wish to have space, once more,

without one. I hope by saying this now, I am giving you time to discern your own way forward. (Sister Anne Julian CSMV, 2008)

In this modest statement Sister Anne Julian underestimated the value of her wardenship for SCK. It provided an example and a recall to the principle of 'being before doing'. During her time as Warden there was less anxious effort to publicise SCK and more attention to pastoral care of scattered and elderly members. Anne Julian had more than once in her life been close to death and was able to help both the movement and its people to look death in the face.

The suggestion that SCK might go on for some time without a Warden was not taken up. A new Warden was at hand. Wendy Robinson had long experience of SCK and was well known to members. She had recently been appointed as one of the movement's trustees and was now the clear and right choice to succeed as Warden. She had first come into contact with SCK when she met Gonville ffrench-Beytagh in the early 1960s. Her talks on 'Exploring Silence' at the 1973 SCK conference, first published in the SCK Newsletter (Robinson, Exploring Silence, 1974) and subsequently by the Sisters of the Love of God (Fairacres), are still in print (Robinson, Exploring Silence, 2013). She was again an invited speaker at the annual conference in 1982 (SCK Central Company, 1982). At the 2007 conference she gave a series of talks about what she called her 'ecumenical journey to Orthodoxy' (Robinson, A Journey to the Russian Orthodox Church, 2007).

Much of Wendy Robinson's professional life had been in the field of mental health. She longed for theologians to provide an adequate theology for this kind of work, but found that she had to struggle with the theology herself (Robinson, The Lost Traveller's Dream, 1995). She was also a spiritual director with a one-to-one ministry which helped many people including clergy. The SCK method was an important part of her work with small groups, much of which she conducted within religious communities. She brought these gifts and skills to her wardenship, continuing and developing the work of Sister Anne Julian in reconciling SCK members with ageing and contemplating death.

It was becoming clear that the central organisation of SCK could no longer be sustained. Since the early years, people in SCK had been looking around for kindred organisations and movements. People had been invited to conferences, joint meetings had been held, articles had been written in the SCK Newsletter, all without lasting results. Now the question again arose of whether there might be a natural successor to which, at least, enquirers could be directed. However, no such successor was found. By the spring of 2013 SCK was without a treasurer and the average age of the remaining office-holders was in the eighties. An open letter from Wendy Robinson, Alison Norman and myself put the situation clearly:

What is God's will for SCK as we go forward into our seventy-first year? As Roger Lloyd used to say, 'If you want to know what is God's will, look at what he is doing already'. The central functions which support the movement – the conference, the newsletter, the central company, the administrative tasks involved in maintaining our charity status – rely on the efforts of a handful of people for whom successors seem hardly to be in sight.

At last year's conference we were already thinking about our spiritual legacy and we encouraged Brian to go on with his book (or books) as a contribution to this. It is the future of waiting upon God in company which is important. SCK companies have faithfully practised waiting upon God over the years and continue to do so; but so do others who choose not to call themselves SCK; and so also may many others in the future. We are convinced that the need is there, even though it may take some time yet before it is fully recognised.

Is the central organisation of SCK really called by God to carry this forward, or is he saying 'well done, you good and faithful servants'? May we even be standing in the way of a new flourishing of groups having a sense of shared vocation ready to wait upon God?

As we look forward to this year's conference as an affirmation of SCK's first seventy years, we feel that God is asking us to give attention to preparing for a good ending for SCK as an organisation. We ask all our members to wait upon God in their companies and at conference to seek his will for our future. (Robinson, Norman, & Bridge, Waiting upon God for the Future, 2013)

In September 2013 the annual conference decided that no conference would be arranged for 2015. The booking had already been made for the 2014 conference at Park Place in Hampshire, the scene of many past SCK conferences. Wendy Robinson had arranged for Dr Rowan Williams, recently retired as Archbishop of Canterbury and now Master of Magdalene College Cambridge, to attend as guest speaker. This was to be the last conference of SCK. Wendy had prepared the movement for it but did not live to see it. She died in December 2013. Her funeral was held in the Anglican surroundings of Exeter Cathedral. It was an Orthodox service attended by clergy, religious and lay people from many different traditions. Speaking at the service, Rowan Williams said:

Wendy enlightened us – she put us in touch with that which enlightens us. She gave us that sense of exploration. Wendy gave without reserve, yet with a sense of reserve unfathomed. Great friendship she gave us, and gave us some glimpse of what God himself is like – who holds nothing back ... and yet is unfathomed.

Wendy enlightened her friends. She lightened their burdens who through her may give thanks for that which she lightened. For she reflected light and we pray that she with eyes enlightened will know the light to which our Lord Jesus Christ has called her. (Norman, Tributes to Wendy Robinson, 2014)

The final conference of the Servants of Christ the King was held in September 2014 at Park Place Pastoral Centre in Hampshire, a favourite venue for SCK conferences over many years. It combined celebration and farewell, resignation and reaffirmation. It was a time for facing reality and making hard decisions. The conference instructed the trustees to expend the remaining funds, giving priority to the publication of this book, and then to wind up the charity. The dozen or so remaining local companies were free to continue independently but there would be no Warden, no Central Company and no Newsletter. Hopes were expressed that new people would discover the value of waiting on God in small groups, though not under the name of The Servants of Christ the King. After all, it was known that some such groups existed already.

It was an ending which also felt like a beginning. The constant underlying theme seemed to be one of reaping and sowing. There was a great harvest to be thankful for and a sense that the gathered seed was already in the ground and ready to spring up in some new form. Even the attendance list seemed to reflect this. There were representatives from every stage of the movement – from Jeannie Yonge who was at the first conference through former members of the 'youth' company and the old Central Company and onwards to the present and some very welcome new faces. And when we read out the 117 names of past members recorded on our 'green leaves' at the memorial service, and later ceremonially burned the leaves, we knew that 'the company of heaven' was also part of the harvest and the seed. (Norman, The 2014 Conference, 2014)

PART II

ADVENTURES IN DISCIPLESHIP

CHAPTER SIX

'A STRANGE AND BEWILDERING EXERCISE'

Waiting on God became and remained the characteristic way, the life and the soul of the Servants of Christ the King. It did not come easily to those who tried to practise it. What was this way, how did it come into being, why did people find it bewildering, and why did SCK persist with it with few modifications despite all the difficulties?

A disciplined structure of waiting on God was introduced early in the first year of SCK's existence and persisted largely unaltered throughout the lifetime of the movement. It was, and still is, adaptable to changes in context and content. Within it small groups can learn, grow in fellowship and decide on corporate action in the service of Christ and the church. It has five essential components: introduction; silence; controlled discussion; open discussion; and recording of decisions made in unanimity. All these are intended to be undertaken within a context of commitment and self-offering, willingness to be open to God-given concerns and readiness to act on decisions which appear to be right 'to the Holy Spirit and to us' (Acts 15:28).

Some groups meeting in this way may already have a God-given concern, whilst others are waiting to learn what such a concern might be for them. At the beginning of each meeting, there is usually some kind of introduction, whether by reading or prayer. This can help the group to recollect its existing concern, or at least its 'concern for a concern'. The introduction is usually undertaken by a group leader, who can be someone appointed for a period by the group or (more often in recent times) any member by rotation within the group. There is sometimes also a brief report of developments since the last meeting, to which several members may contribute. Thus the common concern of the group is submitted to the Holy Spirit to be refined or even totally changed in the repeated alternation of prayer and discussion which takes place over a series of meetings. Each member is committed to making attendance at every meeting a top priority in their lives.

After the introduction to the meeting, the group goes into silence for a predetermined length of time, typically thirty minutes. The silence is not and cannot be programmed, though there will naturally be some influence from the introduction which preceded it. Much and varied advice has been given on what to do in the silence of the SCK meeting, and how to deal with distractions. The actual practice of SCK members has been even more varied than the advice given (Norman, Anthology of SCK members' lives, 2007-08). In general this is seen as a time for prayer, though human frailty does not always live up to the intention. Perhaps three main kinds of prayer can be recognised in the advice which successive SCK leaders have given: the prayer of adoration; the prayer of self-offering; and the prayer of petition whether for the world, for discernment on a particular problem or issue, or for one another. There is a place for all of these, and they may combine and interact in the prayer of simply listening. Olive Parker wrote of the silence in SCK meetings as having the potential to become 'the simple, loving regard of these few disciples who gather round the Master to find how best they can serve him' (Parker, The New Commandment, 1962, p. 22).

Silence is followed by a period of 'controlled discussion'. This is a time in which each member of the group in turn has an opportunity to speak and be heard with attention. Discussion is controlled in that speakers are advised not to comment at this stage on what others have said, and listeners are discouraged from interrupting the speaker. Otherwise there are no rules about the content of what is spoken, though there is usually some expectation that it will have been inspired or at least affected by the prayer of the preceding silence and the common concern of the group.

Next comes open discussion, a time for sifting and sorting of matters raised in the controlled discussion, together with continuing issues which may have been mentioned in the introduction. Gently, the group may move towards 'being of one mind' (Philippians 2:2). Sometimes a further short period of quiet may help to resolve difficulties before the discussion continues.

If the group seems to be ready to agree on some matter, whether great or small, that agreement is tested for unanimity. Unanimous decisions are binding on every member and are recorded, either in writing or in the collective memory of the group. As Roger Lloyd wrote in 1944: '[T]he supreme rule of decision is that there must be no decision – and certainly none which is meant to lead to action – unless and until it is unanimous.'

(Lloyd, The Inspiration of God, 1944, p. 39) We wait on God, and we wait for one another. This can try the patience of those members who want to get on with the job as they see it. But waiting for unanimity strengthens the fellowship of the group and can often result in better decisions. It can encourage the majority to listen to the sometimes prophetic voice of the dissident, can prevent the group from being carried along by one person's enthusiasm, can help the less articulate members of the group to contribute their knowledge, and can often result in a far stronger commitment to action because all have contributed to its initiation. The unanimity rule is an application of Roger Lloyd's maxim 'Being before doing'. Members of the group must wait and pray to be brought to the unity of the spirit before obeying that unity in action.

Some of the groups which influenced the practice of the Servants of Christ the King, such as the First Cell and the Winchester Fellowship, wrote down even minor decisions and placed them on the altar in the final act of their meetings. Members also took it in turns to write a report of their impressions ([Ward], 1937). The practice of writing down and offering the 'findings' of the group at every meeting was continued into SCK (Anon., Waiting upon God, 1945), though this eventually fell into disuse.

Some similarities are apparent between the SCK way of waiting on God and the disciplines of Quaker worship and decision-making. Yet the Servants of Christ the King were wholly Anglican during their first ten years and remained predominantly Anglican long after that. Quaker influence was indirect and had already been filtered and adapted to an Anglican understanding of church and sacraments before SCK began (Lloyd, An Adventure in Discipleship, 1953, p. 122).

* * *

Edmund Morgan was appointed Archdeacon of Winchester in 1936, a year before Roger Lloyd came to Winchester as Diocesan Missioner. The two were soon to become neighbours in the Cathedral Close. Edmund Morgan had met Quakers while he was Warden of the College of the Ascension in Birmingham. The Selly Oak group of colleges had grown up around the Quaker settlement at Woodbrooke, founded in 1903. Other Christian denominations set up colleges in Selly Oak over the following twenty years. Contacts between Christian denominations were encouraged in Selly Oak to an extent not seen until much later elsewhere in Britain. By 1934, feeling that 'more must be done about reunion [of the churches]', Edmund Morgan had brought together a small group from the staff of the colleges to meet fairly regularly over a period, using the Quaker form of worship, sitting in silence together and speaking only when moved by the Holy Spirit. This form of worship was chosen because it did not conflict with that of any other church (Beach & Beach, 1981, pp. 43-4).

Soon after his arrival in the Winchester diocese Edmund Morgan was invited by his spiritual director Reginald Somerset Ward (1881-1962) to become one of the founder members of 'The Cell' (also known as 'The First Cell' and 'A Fellowship in the Gospel'). This was a small group of clergy who felt called together by a shared 'anxiety of the Holy Ghost', desired to be used by God and were 'ready to accept the cost'. They sought to respond to the call prayerfully in a way which would avoid the limitations of what Somerset Ward called 'the committee mind'. The members of the cell, all of them clergy, met for two days at a time, with a chairman chosen by lot for each meeting. Silence in chapel alternated with discussion. The chairman's record of the meeting and of any decisions reached was placed on the altar at the final Eucharist. Although the whole tone of the meeting was Anglican and sacramental, owing much of its form to that of a retreat, there were also significant features in common with Quaker practice. As in the Quaker 'meeting for worship for business', decisions were reached not by majority voting but by unity reached after a combination of silent prayer and discussion. The 'anxiety of the Holy Ghost' which brought cell members together could be recognised as having some similarities to what Quakers call a 'concern', a perceived divine call leading to practical action after prayerful testing in the meeting ([Ward], 1937). This was later taken up in the SCK concept of 'common concern', the basis on which companies were meant to come together.

Although Reginald Somerset Ward strongly discouraged publicity, word got around and other cells began to form on similar lines. One such cell was formed in the Winchester diocese to support the missionary work of SPG. Then in 1941 a cell was formed which brought together the heads of departments at Church House, Winchester, who had previously had little contact with one another. This came to be called the Winchester Fellowship. Roger Lloyd was a member of the new Fellowship and led its first meeting at a 36-hour retreat in May 1941. In notes circulated to members of the cell before the meeting he wrote:

> The purpose of the cell is to live, to receive its life from God to offer its corporate life for God's use, leaving it to God to choose the form in which that life shall be apparent. This means that a cell has to be prepared to appear as a fool for Christ's sake. It may have nothing to point to in the way of results. To the question, what are your plans?

it may have to answer – we have none except to continue to offer the life of the cell for God's use. Those who form the cell must be united by (a) a sense that God is drawing them to this way; (b) a desire to be used, and a readiness to accept the cost ... ; (c) a common concern – in this case could we say? 'The place of the family in God's purpose and its training in living response to that purpose' (Lloyd, Notes for Winchester Fellowship, 1941).

The timetable proposed by Roger Lloyd consisted of two cycles, each of silent prayer, discussion, formulation and record. These were arranged within a structure of daily services of Holy Communion and Evensong. In each cycle half an hour was given to silent prayer, followed immediately by an hour or more of discussion. Then, after a break, those present were asked to spend half an hour in silence and with prayer trying to formulate in their minds and committing to writing any conclusion which seemed to them clear. This led on into a half-hour session for record, in which those present read out any conclusions reached and attempted in subsequent discussions to reach an agreed form of words. No formula was to be accepted unless it was unanimously agreed and sufficiently definite to be of real use as a guide to the opinion and actions of those present.

In the interim constitution and rule of the Servants of Christ the King, the founding conference declared that the foundation of the life of an SCK company was 'waiting upon God in a due alternation of discussion and prayer' (SCK Conference, 1943). This commitment was based on the previous experience of Roger Lloyd, Edmund Morgan and perhaps others. However, neither the obligation nor the form of waiting on God were clearly defined at the conference, though they may have been clear in the minds of some of the founders.

Within a few months a leaflet of guidance was sent out to SCK companies. The pattern of waiting on God had been developed in clergy groups meeting in a retreat setting. The challenge was now to extend it to companies of lay people with no previous experience of this kind, meeting for only a few hours at a time, often in people's homes or (so it was hoped) factories. Although waiting on God was prescribed for all SCK companies, it was not expected to be practised at every meeting. It was suggested that the company wait on God in this way at one meeting in every two or three, with some of the intervening meetings being given to study. Later it would become usual for companies to wait on God at every meeting. The conduct of discussions was formalised, with an initial period of 'controlled discussion' in which each person had the opportunity and encouragement to speak and be heard without interruption or comment. This replaced the reading of individual written statements which had followed the silence in the Winchester Fellowship.

> We should take all the time which may be necessary – a whole meeting if need be – to make sure that a particular subject is allotted to us by God as our common concern.
>
> Once this is done, the company leader is in a position to open the cycle by saying, 'This evening we shall pray about so-and-so.' About this we pray in silence for a given time – perhaps ten or fifteen minutes – and the end of it is announced by the saying of a prayer. We kneel or sit, as comes easier; and we have handy a pencil and paper to write down any thoughts which God may send us. Then, having asked for divine enlightenment and inspiration, we simply think over the problem in a spirit of prayer.
>
> The discussion follows. It is of course a discussion not only about the problem itself, but about the problem *as interpreted by the common experience of praying together about it.* We do not want to discuss the problem academically, but to find out what God is saying about it *to us,* as a fellowship. (Anon., Waiting upon God, 1943)

Much effort was put into giving instruction. People were trained to become group leaders, who would keep boundaries and unobtrusively help the group to move towards unity. Each company was required to have a priest-adviser who would be able to teach the method and who had a power of veto over all company decisions.

It was considered important to make a written record of all agreements reached by the company, however small these might appear to be. According to Roger Lloyd, the record was made and offered to God in the meeting (Lloyd, An Adventure in Discipleship, 1953, p. 57), though some companies recorded and offered their decisions less formally:

> The chairman … sums up the 'findings' and the company goes over to the church to say compline together. At the next meeting the leader reads out the 'findings' which he has drafted at leisure, and with any necessary amendments they are entered in the minute book. (Anon., The Servants of Christ the King, 1949)

The record was important because in the course of a meeting lasting only a couple of hours there would normally be time for only one sequence of prayer – discussion – possible agreement – record. The cycle in which 'prayer and discussion build each other, each giving the appropriate theme for the other' (Lloyd, The Inspiration of God, 1944, p. 39) might be apparent only over an extended period of the group's existence. The record helped to strengthen the sense of continuity between meetings. Regular attendance was strongly enjoined for similar reasons.

* * *

What was strange and bewildering about waiting on God? Beginning his address to the SCK conference in 1944, Edmund Morgan noted that this had been the experience of some companies. Similar difficulties are mentioned in several SCK Newsletters over the next few years. We may be able to infer what some of these difficulties were by reading between the lines of Edmund Morgan's address. He emphasised that waiting on God is an attitude of mind and not just a technique. He warned against a mechanical view of prayer and guidance and instead asked his hearers to learn patience and to train themselves in a belief in 'long-distance guidance'. He gave advice on how to spend the time in the fellowship of silent prayer. He described types of common concern which might bring an SCK company together. He quoted with approval a writer who pointed to our fellowship with other disciples as the place in which we experience our personal relationship to Christ: the fellowship of the Holy Spirit as the organic life of the church.

These points needed explaining in 1944 and are still relevant today. Waiting on God may seem natural and right to people who have been with SCK for a long time, but it is still counter-cultural. Silence has recently been the subject of several popular books, but the majority deal only or mainly with silence enjoyed alone, and in these a tinge of individualism and even consumerism can sometimes be detected. Pervasive technology may give further encouragement to a 'coin-in-the slot' idea of prayer for guidance. Fellowship has become a tired and seemingly outmoded word, and no other word has been able to take its place.

But even when all this is understood, there is something intrinsically strange and bewildering in waiting on God. If we do not feel strangeness and bewilderment we are missing something. By opening ourselves to God's creative energy we are venturing in faith into the dark, into unknowing. Silence cannot be programmed, whatever advice may be given about how to 'use' it (and there is plenty of advice on this in the SCK literature). We wait, putting our own hopes and plans aside, 'for hope would be hope for the wrong thing' (Eliot, East Coker, 1940). In the waiting, as Edmund Morgan warned, we shall inevitably be convicted of sin. We are not in control.

Waiting on the Holy Spirit can be full of perils, for not every spirit is of God. SCK provided some safeguards, including the requirement for every company to have a priest-adviser and the commitment of every member to receive Holy Communion regularly in their parish church. The rule of unanimity in all decisions and the subjection of these decisions to the right of veto of the priest-adviser could also help companies from going off the rails.

Even in unanimity and with the best advice, groups can reach wrong decisions (Parker, The New Commandment, 1962, p. 25). There is also the ever-present possibility of false unanimity (Bridge, Waiting on God, 2013, p. 24). The unanimity which is sought in waiting on God is an honest, true and deep unanimity of free persons. But there are other kinds of unanimity. There is a unanimity of intimidation. We sometimes read of dictators re-elected with ninety-nine per cent of the votes in an election, and shake our heads. There is a more subtle false unanimity, that of deference. Even among friends and family we can experience the paradox when everyone is trying to please everyone else, yet no one has the courage to question whether this is the best course of action (or inaction). The pushy need to learn restraint and the timid need to learn, with encouragement, to let their reservations be known. Honest, true and deep unanimity does not always come naturally. With good leadership, the discipline of controlled discussion within a regular practice of waiting on God can encourage everyone to listen and be heard.

The experience of waiting on God in company can indeed be strange and bewildering. But it gives practical embodiment to the belief that life in Christ is lived in free and equal fellowship. It strengthens commitment to one another, yet helps to guard against the danger that the group may override or disregard the God-given individuality of each person. It is a high calling and it can be demanding. Seventy years of experience have shown that it is practicable for lay people who are willing to commit themselves. It has been the heart and soul of the Servants of Christ the King. It is adaptable to many different circumstances and situations and could be a way forward for many Christian groups seeking to serve the Lord and their neighbours.

CHAPTER SEVEN

COMMON CONCERN

Common concern is understood in SCK as a call by the Holy Spirit to become involved in some particular aspect of the world, a call felt by each member of a group and through which that group is brought together as a fellowship. As a group continues to meet and to wait on God, its common concern may be worked out, clarified or radically changed. It may begin as no more than a feeling that 'something ought to be done' together with a willingness to respond ('here am I, send me') and to join with others as a group to work on that response, becoming 'here are we, send us'.

Roger Lloyd regarded shared work as essential to the life of an SCK company. From the outset, each company needed to make 'an act of faith by which they believe that God has a work for them, as a group, to do' (Lloyd, The Inspiration of God, 1944, p. 38). Only by waiting on God could the group discover what that work was. The author of the earliest SCK leaflet on waiting on God (probably Roger Lloyd himself) was hopeful that such a common concern would quickly emerge, even for a group which started with no more than a 'unanimous perplexity':

> It will very soon be found that one subject appeals to all, and that is the subject to choose. It will probably be related to the work of evangelism, which is after all the common concern of every company in the Order. We have to wait upon God in prayer to ask him to inspire us to know what part of the whole work of bringing others to Christ is given to us as the task of our company. (Anon., Waiting upon God, 1943)

Edmund Morgan made it clear that companies were to offer to be used in whatever way God might direct them (what he was later to describe as 'offering ourselves blind'), but added that 'experience shows that no company can continue to offer its life to God in this way unless it is bound together by a common concern'. He defined common concern as 'the reflection of that bit of God's love for the world which is drawing a company together' (Morgan, Waiting upon God: An Explanation, 1944).

Corporate waiting on God, as understood by the founders of SCK, is based on a common concern of the group. This common concern informs the alternation of prayer and discussion and is in turn shaped and re-shaped by group decisions and their outcomes. For a common concern to bind a group together as servants, it needs to be definite and specific. It gives a shared and explicit meaning to the existence of the group. Without such a common concern, meetings have nothing to bite on and the group is in danger of becoming no more than a religious club (Parker, The New Commandment, 1962, p. 28).

This was the original vision of Roger Lloyd and Edmund Morgan, later to be reaffirmed by Olive Parker and Gonville ffrench-Beytagh and re-stated again and again over the years (Bridge, Waiting on God, 2013). It was always the custom at SCK conferences for companies to report on their life, work and concerns. Roger Lloyd remarked on the diffidence with which many of these reports were given, beginning 'we really have nothing exciting to report' but going on to refer to all kinds of Christian service to which the company had been led.

In the early years, SCK companies provided support for local 'permanent mission', proposed and helped to inaugurate a parish conference, and helped to fill in some of the gaps during a long inter-regnum in their parish. One company sponsored a company member through college to train as a religious education teacher, another attempted (unsuccessfully) to set up a housing association and health centre, while another gave long-term help to a troubled family. Later examples included helping to establish an old people's home, supporting and helping to staff a counselling centre which had been started by the local Methodists, trying to rescue a youth club which was facing closure, and supporting hospital or prison chaplaincy by prayer and visiting. In one city several companies shared a common concern for persecuted Christians, with each company informing itself and arranging its own scheme of intercessions, co-ordinated by a quarterly meeting of leaders. Later, several companies found their common concerns in the housing of elderly people. An outstanding example of this was in Winchester, where a disused stable block in the Cathedral Close was converted into retirement flats and cottages, creating an SCK community (Anon., Paternoster House, 1997).

Overseas companies were led by concern into further areas of need. One felt called to create opportunities for African and European Anglicans to meet socially and on equal terms, which had not been considered possible before in that colonial setting. A company in Hong Kong became involved in relieving need in poor areas of that territory, including buying a fishing boat for one of the villages.

Many of these concerns were of their time and would not fit into today's world. Housing and social services, in which many SCK companies were once involved, have become highly professionalised. British colonial rule is almost entirely a thing of the past and expatriate missionaries are far fewer in number. Companies were led to new concerns, some arising out of new needs and opportunities in a changing society, others out of the new perspectives of company members as they themselves grew older. Several companies developed common concerns for homelessness in their local areas. Another recurring theme was loneliness: for example a company set up a local prayer link with elderly and housebound church members to prevent them from being cut off from the churches they once attended. In another company each member undertook 'to visit someone we would not normally visit'.

The original expectation in SCK was that every local company would start with at least an embryonic common concern, or would soon receive one if it really offered itself in God's service. Yet many companies, especially those which had started out without an explicit common concern, did not seem to find one. Many possible reasons were suggested for this. Some companies, whether through modesty or ambition, thought that the small piece of service in which they were engaged was not spectacular enough to be counted. Such service, however humble or impractical it might seem to members of these companies, was recognisable as common concern, and with leadership and encouragement they could be brought to see it as such. Some groups, feeling that a 'real' concern should have quick and tangible results, expected short-term guidance leading straight into action and underestimated the long-term and often hidden value of their prayer. Perhaps some also undervalued the divine discomfort (described by Reginald Somerset Ward as 'the anxiety of the Holy Ghost') which might for a long time remain no more than a feeling that something is wrong in the world, requiring prayer, study and exploration.

Whilst common concern was being put forward as the basis on which companies came together and waited on God, there was a growing feeling that many companies were not ready to be used by being put into Spirit-led action. 'Being before doing' became a byword in SCK. Roger Lloyd and others began to suggest that the process of becoming people whom God could use could take a long time. This did not rule out the need for a common concern for a company during its growth into Christ. Roger Lloyd wrote in 1957:

> [A] company offers its corporate life to God through the Holy Spirit, and at the same time, and paradoxically, offers itself as it is in order to receive from God the divine life and power to become what it should. All this is vital. Activity is purely secondary. There must be some activity because we must never become satisfied by quiescence. But often enough the activity will look like stillness, just prayer, discipline, fellowship, mutual dependence, and joy. This is what our companies do. Their 'good works' follow from this. (Lloyd, But What Do These Companies Actually Do?, 1957)

Some companies seem to have lost patience with this slow process. Others, less naturally inclined to activism, could have lost sight of the practical. Julian Rudd re-asserted the importance of both when he spoke at the 1960 SCK conference:

> [Being formed into Christ corporately] does not of course mean that we have to wait until the company or the parish has grown into oneness before we can set about the tasks that God gives us to do. Individually while it is true that we cannot be used fully until we are sanctified, yet we are sanctified by being used. So with the company. The degree to which it can be used depends on the quality of its corporate life, but that corporate life is deepened and unified by the tasks which the company undertakes. While it may be true to say that the first task of the church is to be the church, and that the first task of the company is to be the company, yet in practice the church can never be the church and the company will never be the company, unless it sets about tackling the jobs that lie to hand. It is as we set about our common tasks, provided that we are impelled by a desire to draw men to Christ, that we shall grow together and our growing unity will make each company a more effective member of the body through which Christ acts. (Rudd, 1960, p. 10)

It came to be understood, at least by the leadership of SCK, that companies which fully offered themselves to Christ's service were obeying a 'vocation to an undisclosed purpose'. An implication of this was that there could be a large gap between the purpose of the company as God saw it and the common concern which the company thought it had at the time.

If [companies] offer themselves, they will be used, and they have no right to expect that they will be told how they are being used. That is what makes it so difficult to assess what is the condition of the movement or of any particular company. From the outside, a company may appear to be doing all manner of wildly exciting and worth-while things, but from God's point of view the real value of that company may lie in something quite different. Or it may be doing nothing at all, because it has never really offered itself to be used. (Rudd, 1960, p. 7)

It is not surprising that, as Olive Parker observed in 1962, companies could experience genuine difficulties in knowing what work they should be undertaking together. Some simply gave up the search for a common concern. Others saw their main purpose as supporting members of their company who had especially demanding lives and responsibilities. In 1973 Alison Norman visited a number of companies and individual people who had been involved in SCK. She wrote: 'Almost every company which I visited said, more or less apologetically, that they did not really have a common concern or that they were only an intercession and bible study group and perhaps therefore not proper SCK at all.' When Alison Norman interviewed sixty-two SCK members in 2007-8, none of those still in ordinary SCK companies reported an active common concern of the traditional sort.

Although many companies did not claim to have a common concern, the SCK leadership and literature continued to stress its importance. This engendered feelings of guilt in some companies and may have led to others dropping out altogether. Members of companies needed to ask themselves from time to time 'Why are we here together?' and the answer was expected to be 'Because God has called us together in his service'. If that service did not seem to be revealed over a period of time, a group might begin to ask whether God had really called them together. There might also be a guilty feeling in some members of the group that they had not truly offered themselves and had not been open to the anxieties and needs which God had been placing before them all the time.

Part of the problem arose from the word 'concern'. This had been borrowed from the Quakers but given a somewhat different meaning by SCK. According to Quaker experience, a 'concern' is given to an individual and is

... a special inward calling to carry out a particular service. It is characterised by a feeling of having been directly called by God and by an imperative to act. (Britain Yearly Meeting of the Religious Society of Friends, 2013, 13.02)

The role of the Quaker meeting is to foster, test and support the concerns of its individual members. Some instances of corporate action, such as the creation of Friends Ambulance Unit during the First World War, had begun with what the historian and archivist Edward Milligan called 'concern developing through corporate and mutually dependent worship of God'. But even here there was heart-searching as to whether every part of the work was being done under individual concern by every worker in the field (Milligan, 1948, p. 92).

In general, what Quakers call 'concern' is laid by God on some but by no means all people; it is given individually; it is clear and specific; and it involves particular action. By contrast, 'common concern', as understood by the founders of SCK, was expected to be given to groups. Perhaps it would initially be given in embryo to several individuals so as to bring a group together, but thereafter it would be given corporately. The common concern of a group was not necessarily clear at first, and it was always provisional. It might involve particular action, but it might be no more than a feeling that something was not as it should be and that the group was being called to become involved in it in some way. The SCK concept of 'common concern' evolved, after all, from the 'anxiety of the Holy Ghost' which Reginald Somerset Ward had seen as the basis of The Cell.

In an article published in 1957, Roger Lloyd expressed his regret that the word 'concern' had caused confusion in SCK companies and suggested that they think instead of 'vocation'. The idea of vocation brought together both the calling to be a member of an SCK company and a calling to undertake some particular work for the kingdom. Every member had accepted a vocation when making or renewing the membership promise.

> Whenever someone is admitted to membership of the Servants of Christ the King he is asked the question, 'Do you believe that you are called by God into this membership, and will you accept its obligations for the next twelve months?', and to this he must answer, 'I do believe it and I do accept them.' ... That is to say, he accepts two things. First, he accepts the principle of vocation as applying not only to the church itself but also to his membership of a particular society within the church. Secondly, he accepts the principle that the same vocation, coming from the same source which is God, may be either lifelong, as in the case of the church, or temporary, as in the case of SCK, or both. From the beginning therefore, one condition of membership has been the acceptance of a divine vocation to it. (Lloyd, Vocation in SCK, 1957)

Roger Lloyd argued that to acknowledge membership of SCK to be a vocation was to acknowledge that vocation was for all and not for just a few. God's calling was not just for special occasions. It went on all the time. There were little vocations to particular duties as well as bigger vocations to a whole way of life.

> A sense of divine vocation is, or ought to be, the universal experience of all mankind. At present it is not, since all the world is not yet Christian. But for the convinced and practising Christian there can surely be no doubt whatever. If the things he believes about God are true, it follows automatically that God will call every one of us, not once only but constantly, to serve him by placing ourselves in this pattern of life or in that, by living in a particular kind of way, and by undertaking this, that, or the other specific duty. Vocation is the voice of God, claiming each one of us, calling us to be and do something of our own for him, and sending us to undertake something for his kingdom in the power of the Holy Spirit. (Lloyd, Vocation in SCK, 1957)

God's calling, the argument continued, was not only to individuals but also to Christian institutions and to the church as a whole. What SCK meant by 'common concern' was just another way of describing this calling or vocation when it came to a group of people living out their Christian discipleship together.

> If vocation is the experience of individual Christians, so it is part of the life and character of the institutions through which we live out our Christian discipleship. The church herself is called of God to fulfil his purpose for the world, and so are all the handmaids of the church which help her to fulfil this or that part of her total purpose. God's calling to the church, and to the subordinate society within the church, is what gives them their distinctive character. To use the Quaker language, which SCK deliberately adopted but which has caused a good deal of confusion in the past, our vocation is our common concern. Identify the one and the other is then automatically defined. (Lloyd, Vocation in SCK, 1957)

Roger Lloyd's argument proceeds from the sense of calling of an individual into membership of SCK to the reality of God's constant calling into particular duties and service; from the calling of individuals to the calling of the church; and from there to the general and particular calling of all the 'handmaids of the church' including SCK and its companies.

Even if the outlines of this argument are accepted, it does not follow that every group of persons calling themselves Christian must be conscious of God's calling to some particular purpose. Groups come together for all sorts of different reasons, which may not be apparent even to members of the group itself. A sense of being called may be mistaken both as to the source and the nature of the calling. Some groups have a discipline, such as SCK's waiting on God, which helps them to become more sensitised to God's will. But even, and perhaps especially, these groups will come up against the deep mystery of the will of God. As John Henry Newman wrote:

> God has created me to do him some definite service; He has committed some work to me which he has not committed to another. I have my mission – I never may know it in this life, but I shall be told it in the next. (Newman, 1893)

None of this is to say that God does not communicate with us at all. But our consciousness of this communication is limited. Even when a group feels that it has a defined task, something else equally or even more important may be going on at the same time (Norman, Thirty-Six Hours, 1975, p. 14).

Moreover it seems that when God claims us it is often by way of the 'anxiety of the Holy Ghost' – a feeling which will not go away that something needs to be done, without any clarity as to what that something is. That we are left to work it out for ourselves shows God's profound respect for our creativity and free will.

SCK literature and teaching continued to assert the importance of common concern in the life of SCK companies. The language used and the examples given tended to emphasise tasks and visible action. This is seen particularly strongly in Gonville ffrench-Beytagh's description of the SCK practice of waiting on God as being designed to 'explode into action' (ffrench-Beytagh, Advice on Waiting upon God, 1972), though in a later article he drew back somewhat from 'explode' (ffrench-Beytagh, Second Thoughts, 1973). Groups which did not see themselves as being involved in significant action could easily become disheartened. They might continue as SCK but with a guilty conscience, or declare themselves to be something other than SCK, or give up altogether. Some groups may indeed have been right to disband, if their work was done or if they concluded that their members could better serve the kingdom of Christ in some other way. But others may have been needlessly discouraged, not seeing the value of their existence. 'Leavening the lump' does not have the ring of a mission statement for a group and is essentially done unawares.

According to George Willis, an experienced group practitioner and founder of several SCK companies, all small face-to-face groups need a definable task (Norman, Thirty-Six Hours, 1975, p. 13). Although 'common concern' may have been found an unsatisfactory description, something does seem to be needed to motivate the cycle of prayer and discussion in which an SCK company waits on God – some kind of exposure to some part of a world in need of redemption, even if no action seems to be made clear and there is only a sense of shared bewilderment. Without this, all but the most dedicated companies are in danger of becoming flabby and self-satisfied: forgetful hearers of the word who behold themselves but then go their way and lose the vision (James 1:23-5).

CHAPTER EIGHT

THE EVANGELICAL TENSION

Throughout his life Roger Lloyd gave a very high priority to evangelism. He was the son of an industrialist and his particular concern was for bringing Christianity into the world of work and workers. Strongly influenced by William Temple, he became a local organiser for the Industrial Christian Fellowship while serving as a curate in the Manchester diocese. In a letter to the *Manchester Guardian* in 1925 he invited young business men to a meeting with a view to starting a study group on Christianity and economics (Lloyd, The Industrial Christian Fellowship, 1925). As a young vicar in a distressed Lancashire cotton town in the 1930s he was responsible for initiating and leading the organisation of a mission in his parish. The planning and preparation of the mission took up a large part of his time and energy for a whole year. He wrote up the experience of what he described as this 'spiritual adventure' (Lloyd, Crown Him Lord of All, 1936). When he moved to Winchester in 1937, it was as Diocesan Missioner. There he met and became a close friend and neighbour of Edmund Morgan, who was to become an important influence in the development of the Servants of Christ the King. Edmund Morgan and Roger Lloyd later co-edited a book of essays entitled *The Mission of the Anglican Communion* (Morgan & Lloyd, The Mission of the Anglican Communion, 1948).

At the same time as SCK began its existence, others were also recognising a need for a fresh approach to the spreading of the gospel. Following a resolution of the General Assembly of the Church of England in 1943, the Archbishops of Canterbury and York set up a Commission on Evangelism under the chairmanship of Christopher Chavasse, Bishop of Rochester. The commission's report came out in 1945 under the title *Towards the Conversion of England* (Commission on Evangelism, 1945).

If Roger Lloyd had hoped for inspiration from the report, he was disappointed. It was well received in many parts of the church, but for him it was, as he wrote later, 'a long and heavy piece of work which was without visible result'. He accepted much of the analysis in the report, though he felt that it only stated clearly what everyone who had studied the subject already knew. But he saw in it no recognition of the new theology typified by the writings of Dietrich Bonhoeffer, no contribution from the world of the working-class, and no plan, only suggestions that this or that experiment might be tried (Lloyd, The Church of England 1900-1965, 1966, pp. 473-4).

Although Roger Lloyd was committed to the evangelistic imperative in an industrial age, his writings show increasing awareness of the difficulties of that mission. In 1947, in an article in the SCK Newsletter, he wrote: 'Never since SCK began have we quite succeeded in finding a really satisfactory definition of our evangelistic purpose.' In the same article, he compared the experience of SCK with the Mission de Paris, quoting with approval the statement in the book which launched that movement (Godin & Daniel, 1943): 'It seems that the task of a truly popular Catholic mission must be to uncover and identify every human community which exists, and to form within each one of them a Christian cell which, with the aid of a priest, shall become a radiating and radiant community.' Roger Lloyd commented 'This *is* SCK' and added:

> It is very interesting to see how so many Christian minds, starting from different points of view, are converging on the same point, and that the very point which SCK has had in mind from the beginning. Our point was and is that the present gulf between the church and so many of the people can only be bridged by the laity, organised in small groups or companies within the communities which need to be converted. At the very beginning this is what we hoped to do, but so far we have not been able to do it. In the past five years we have had a few companies in spheres like factories, hospitals, the army, the RAF, but nine out of ten of our SCK companies have been formed in already Christian spheres in parishes, or in Christian colleges; and to-day there are none at work within a really secular community, not one which is so placed that it can do here what MM. Godin and Daniel declare is the vital work to be done in France.

He concluded with a call to SCK to reconsider its vocation to workplace evangelism.

All this reflection was provoked by the book I began by quoting, and by my astonished gratification that two French priests should have judged that the SCK method was the primary instrument which they need in France. It has made me very conscious of the fact that SCK is not at present at work in any really secular sphere, and rather uneasy about it, and I believe that this ought to be the chief subject of our prayers and discussion at the next conference. (Lloyd, SCK Newsletter, 1947, pp. 1-4)

Roger Lloyd was always critical of evangelistic methods, including his own. He had preached from a soapbox early in his career (Lloyd, Crown Him Lord of All, 1936, p. 45), but later wrote that oratory was useless for appealing to the working class, who were 'almost completely proofed against oratory of every kind' (Lloyd, The Church and the Artisan Today, 1952, p. 60). Although he recognised that anyone coming newly into the church would find the services difficult to understand, he was unsympathetic to those who wanted to change the language and actions in order to bring people in. He was initially enthusiastic for the Mission de Paris and the French worker-priest movement, but later came to regard their example as irrelevant for the British situation. He believed that the undoubted heroism of these priests would not and could not remove the class barrier between priest and workman (Lloyd, The Church and the Artisan Today, 1952, pp. 91-3).

Roger Lloyd dedicated his book on this subject to 'SCK, who stimulated my thought about this and gladly suffered me to expound it'. In it he described the problems of evangelising what he regarded as the new dominant class, the urban factory workers (whom he called 'the artisans'). The political and social analysis of the book now looks extremely dated, with an expectation that most workers would continue to be employed in industrial mass-production and that the trades unions would continue to be the dominant force in British life and politics. However, this is how it must have seemed to many people at the time. Within these assumptions, Roger Lloyd proceeded to consider and reject many of the ideas of evangelism which had already been tried or suggested. His conclusion was that 'the artisan can only be loved into the kingdom of God' (Lloyd, The Church and the Artisan Today, 1952, p. 61), yet only in the final eight pages do we find a few positive ideas for putting this into practice. The feeling which comes over from reading the book is one of impotence and frustration.

From time to time Roger Lloyd expressed his disappointment with SCK, which he had seen as an instrument for evangelism capable of reaching places where the clergy could not reach, but which seemed to have stalled before making a significant impact except in a few places.

> [T]he movement grows with terrible slowness, while the pace of the life of the world which it was designed to help to redeem moves ever faster. If you count progress by the number of the companies, SCK has been practically stationary for at least two years. And though we have had this out at one conference after another, I am still unconvinced that we are doing all we might for evangelism. (Lloyd, The Future of SCK, 1951)

In Roger Lloyd's book *An Adventure in Discipleship* (Lloyd, An Adventure in Discipleship, 1953) two out of the nine chapters were concerned with evangelism. The title of the seventh chapter was 'The Evangelistic Tension'. It recounted how by 1948 it was already clear that SCK and its companies were not doing the directly evangelistic work which they had originally been designed for. The hope and intention of setting up an SCK company in 'every factory, every regiment, every institution' had simply not come to pass, and those companies which were flourishing were based in parishes and working most effectively in the pastoral sphere. The tension of which he wrote was between two different ideas of evangelism: that of 'the effort of the faithful to convert the unfaithful' and that of 'the work of loving people into the kingdom of God'. The 1948 SCK conference recognised the value of the first but concluded that the work of SCK lay primarily in the second.

Having described this 'evangelical tension' in chapter seven, Roger Lloyd went on in the following chapter to claim that the dilemma was unreal. Parish-based fellowship could after all reach out effectively to the unchurched. He looked to the example of Ipswich, where Canon Richard Babington had been promoting the growth of SCK companies, beginning with local clergy. The clergy companies had 'permanent local mission' as their common concern, and as the first stage of this set out to establish SCK lay companies within their congregations. The lay companies, though separate and autonomous and each having their own common concern, were encouraged to participate in the wider concern of local mission and did so in a variety of ways including house coffee mornings, pub visitations and meetings with foremen and shop stewards from local factories.

The example of Ipswich was clearly considered outstanding at the time and was not necessarily typical. It has some features in common with the 'ripples spreading outwards' described by Canon Stephen Verney (yet another Diocesan Missioner) in the Coventry diocese in the 1960s (Verney, 2010, p. 117).

How far did others share Roger Lloyd's continuing vision of SCK as being an instrument of evangelism? He saw this as a kind of super-concern of the movement, within which each company would find its own local common concern. It is not easy to discover how SCK members and local companies saw it, since the SCK Newsletter and other publications were produced by the Warden and Secretary and most of the articles were written by Roger Lloyd himself. But there are some indications that not all companies saw evangelism as their priority, as for example when Central Company felt it necessary in 1959 to issue a statement recalling companies to 'the primary concern for evangelism' (SCK Central Company, 1959).

Richard Babington, whose evangelistic work in Ipswich Roger Lloyd had so much admired, succeeded him in the wardenship of SCK in 1961. He soon made clear his view that SCK companies could not be committed to any kind of super-concern of the whole movement, not even evangelism. Waiting on God in local companies was the main purpose of SCK and its results could not be pre-empted or pre-programmed.

> By waiting upon God I mean the whole process, corporate silent prayer, discussion and when necessary decision. Out of this waiting upon God many things may come, experiments in other forms of prayer, study, friendship and the call to action. A common concern or many concerns may emerge. Nevertheless waiting upon God is surely an end in itself and not just a means to an end. We cannot use God as a means to any end, not even our plans for the conversion of England. He may have quite different plans. We shall be on the right lines if we 'contemplate and pass on to others the things contemplated'. (Babington, Waiting upon God, 1963)

But is not to 'contemplate and pass on to others the things contemplated' also a form of evangelism? Christ told the apostles to go out and be heralds of the good news to the whole creation (Mark 16:15); and to go out and 'disciple' the nations (Matthew 28:19). He told them that they were the salt of the earth and the light of the world (Matthew 5:13-14); and that they would be his witnesses (Acts 1:8). Saint Paul recognised that an evangelical imperative had been laid on him: 'Woe to me if I do not evangelise' (1 Corinthians 9:16). 'Evangelise' is often translated as 'preach the gospel', but means much more than that, unless 'preach' is taken in a wider sense than just oratory. Paul acted on the evangelical imperative by public speaking, certainly, but also by teaching and writing, and by his sufferings. For him and for many of the early Christians this suffering was to death: so much so that being a martyr (the Greek word for 'witness') came to mean dying for Christ. We see in Saint Paul how adaptable a great evangelist could be. The common factor in evangelism is carrying something of Christ into the world, whether by word, by action, or simply by being there and taking the consequences.

The founders of SCK envisaged the conversion of English society by infiltration. Small groups of Christians would change the world of work by living in it. They would do this without publicity, because this kind of infiltration implies a degree of secrecy (Lloyd, An Adventure in Discipleship, 1953, pp. 95-6). This was the plan on which SCK was built. But things did not go according to plan. When this became clear, it was hoped that SCK would be an instrument for deepening the life of parishes, a necessary preparation for any kind of going out into the world. In the words of the statement issued by the 1951 conference:

> The evangelistic purpose of SCK is in fact to produce in the Church the essential pre-conditions of evangelism, without which no bearing of witness in the world can have its proper effect. (SCK Conference, 1951, p. 4)

Some parish-based companies became involved in explicit evangelistic work, with a common concern for 'permanent neighbourhood mission'. But service to neighbours, which had always been the main feature of the concerns of most SCK companies, was increasingly recognised as being part of God's mission. This type of witness needed to be for the most part unselfconscious. It would have been mistaken and wrong to measure its value by the number of known converts: mistaken because what God does through our lives and actions is often not seen by us; wrong because striving for visibility ministers to our pride and sense of self-sufficiency.

After the death of Roger Lloyd there was less talk of evangelism in SCK. There was still a basic hope and expectation, at least in the leadership of SCK, that companies which waited on God would find themselves propelled out into the world by a common concern. Some companies were indeed led into corporate action. But waiting on God faithfully and with patience led others to a gradual deepening of love for God and neighbour from which evangelical consequences could follow. If the besetting temptation of evangelism by preaching is Pharisaism, that of evangelism by being is lethargy. We shall never know what went on in the recesses of people's hearts, but at least some companies do seem to have been a leaven in their local lump (Rudd, 1960, p. 7). This kind of unselfconscious evangelism takes us back to Roger Lloyd's original vision of the social dimension of conversion. As he wrote in 1944: 'The characteristic method of the Church in fact is that of the play of one community upon and within another.' (Lloyd, The Inspiration of God, 1944, p. 70)

A sign of change can be seen in the publication of a leaflet intended for bulk distribution to parishes and general enquirers (Anon., S.C.K., 1962). From the first moves towards public recognition in the commissioning of *An Adventure in Discipleship*, SCK had by now moved on to promoting itself. Olive Parker wrote passionately about waiting on God in company as a way of Christian life – perhaps even *the* way of Christian life. The appeal was to people who were already Christians and church members, and the task was not in the first instance to go out and convert others but to live more fully as Christians. Waiting on God was not in itself the good news of the kingdom, but was a working out of that good news and a source of strength for taking it into the world. As Secretary, Olive Parker was active in taking the message of SCK out to the churches. Some younger members were deeply impressed by her vision, but many companies seem not to have shared it or at any rate not to have acted on it. At the 1964 conference, Olive Parker expressed regret about 'the reluctance to proclaim SCK as a way of life which we are proud to follow and need others to share with us'. She continued:

> As I deal with the correspondence that comes to me, I am often puzzled by the ambivalent attitude of our people. On the one hand, they will tell you of the value to them of SCK and of the joy that has come to them in company life. Yet they seem to make no effort to bring other companies into being. Sometimes they have tried and failed and, instead of setting about to find out what is wrong with our presentation of SCK, they appear to have decided that it is not right to present it at all. They seem to expect that SCK companies should come into being without conscious effort on their part but will be generated spontaneously and leap up into full life of their own accord.
>
> Are we or are we not proud to belong to the Servants of Christ the King? Why are we all so cagey at talking about SCK even when we have an eager audience? Various respectable reasons have been put forward when I have raised this sort of question. Beneath them lies, I suspect, our own vagueness in knowing to what we are committed and what we are about. (Parker, Call to Commitment, 1964, pp. 6-7)

Although the SCK way was presented as a model of Christian life in community, SCK companies never moved towards becoming cell churches, either as 'pure cells' (free-standing worshipping communities) or as local communities of a 'meta church' (worshipping communities coming together from time to time for celebration in a larger community). Even after the movement renounced its solely Anglican basis in 1964, the typical company continued to be based in an Anglican parish in which most of the company's members were already worshippers. Some hoped that SCK would draw unchurched and dechurched people into company membership, becoming a spiritual haven for people who needed an alternative to church. But this was a minority view within SCK and was hardly seen at all in practice.

CHAPTER NINE

BELOVED COMMUNITIES

Intentional communities living a common life under a rule have had a place in the Christian church since the early centuries. Many types of residential monastic community developed and co-existed, mainly within the Orthodox and Roman Catholic churches. New types of intentional community, large and small, came into being in the twentieth century within and across both Catholic and Protestant traditions (Bonhoeffer, 1954) (Wyon, 1963).

Small groups have been an important part of church life since the time of the apostles. Some were called to undertake a common task, others were held together by geographical constraints when there were few Christians in a particular place. Some were seeking concealment under persecution, others simply felt called to a shared life of prayer and obedience. The apostles themselves were brought together by the Lord's own direct calling and appointment.

The original concept of SCK was not one of residential community. Members were expected to go on living in their own homes and working in their existing occupations, meeting regularly in companies but often not seeing one another for days or even weeks at a time. Nevertheless the movement started life as an Order and continued, at least into the 1960s, to attempt to adapt monastic rule and discipline to its own vision. Some SCK members were also associated with other intentional communities including the Iona Community or Third Orders such as Franciscan Tertiaries. SCK itself maintained connection with other intentional communities through NACCAN (National Association of Christian Communities and Networks) and its successors (Vincent, 2011).

Nonetheless, for some years SCK had its own residential company, started by three members who met at the Exeter conference in 1961. It came into being in 1962, located in Mile End in east London at the request of a local vicar who needed support in his parish, and moving to a larger house in the same area in 1965. Although the residential company came to an end in 1969, the house continued to be a significant place for SCK. It was home for Gonville ffrench-Beytagh in his last years, and it is still the meeting place for the one surviving London company.

Although almost all SCK companies lacked the physical proximity and interdependence of residential communities, they were still capable of bringing people into close fellowship through their limitation on numbers (never more than twelve people in a company) and commitment to meeting regularly.

A year after retiring from the wardenship of SCK, Roger Lloyd gave a talk at the annual conference about small groups in English church history. He started in the sixteenth century with the Protestant reformers who met at the White Horse Tavern in Cambridge and continued, though in less detail, into the nineteenth.

> The late seventeenth and the early eighteenth centuries constitute the first golden age in English history of Christian discipleship through the small group. The second golden age we are experiencing ourselves. (Lloyd, Chapters from an Unwritten History, 1963, pp. 6-7)

The greater part of the talk was about the work of one man:

> ... Anthony Horneck, a German by birth, who became chaplain of the Savoy Chapel in 1671 and stayed there till he died in 1697. Of all those who, through the centuries, have had to do with the small group movement in the Church of England, he is certainly the great example, and perhaps the patron saint. He was a mystic, a high churchman, and a sacramentalist. He prayed for long hours each day. (Lloyd, Chapters from an Unwritten History, 1963, p. 7)

Roger Lloyd divided the many different small group movements into three categories, and saw all three types in movements of the late seventeenth century.

> The first and certainly the purer type come together simply in order to get from each other the mutual society, help and comfort in the spiritual life. They have no propagandist purpose whatever. They do not set out to be busily officious in the reformation of other men. They keep themselves as hidden as they can and for as long as they can. The [second] type come together with a definitely propagandist purpose, and are burdened with an itch to reform other men, even against

their will. They do not want to be hidden. They are always in some degree revolutionary. Inevitably they become self-righteous. (Lloyd, Chapters from an Unwritten History, 1963, p. 6)

[T]here is a third classic form ... the association of a few able Christian men who come together with the clear purpose of getting a specific job done, which no doubt seems as good to the Holy Ghost as to them. It was by just such associations that SPCK and SPG were founded and nurtured through their difficult infant days. (Lloyd, Chapters from an Unwritten History, 1963, p. 12)

The range of Roger Lloyd's historical survey was deliberately limited. There was no reference to Protestant pietist groups before Wesley, or Quaker meetings, or residential communities, or monasticism. He began with the Reformation. All of the groups mentioned were open to the laity, all had some connection with the Church of England, and all were urban. Roger Lloyd was thinking only of movements which could be seen as precursors of the Servants of Christ the King. His rejection of the propagandist type of small group movement can be seen as a warning to SCK companies. His first and third types, respectively for mutual support in the spiritual life and for undertaking specific tasks in accordance with the Holy Spirit, correspond to important aspects of the Servants of Christ the King. It seems that the purpose of the talk was not only to tell a story about the past, but to reassure SCK members that they were not alone. It was an assertion of the legitimacy of SCK companies in the face of the challenges which they had always faced from some parish clergy.

When Roger Lloyd called the twentieth century the second golden age of the small group in Christian discipleship, he seems to have been thinking primarily of so-called cell groups. The growth of these groups in the 1930s was, according to Roger Lloyd's book on the Church of England in the twentieth century, quite unorganised and spontaneous (Lloyd, The Church of England 1900-1965, 1966, p. 381). Some originated from social activism, others from evangelistic endeavour, others from opposition to rigid church structures, others from a reading of the bible which saw many examples of the inspiration of the Holy Spirit being given corporately to small groups rather than to individuals. Some Christians looked at the way in which communist cells infiltrated, or were supposed to infiltrate, every aspect of social and working life, and hoped that the church might be able to emulate the supposed success if not all the methods of the communists.

However, reasoned criticisms could be levelled at every one of these types of cell, depending on one's theological and ecclesiological position and social outlook. Parish clergy who had come up against one type of small group might be suspicious of any kind of small group within their congregations. At the same time, other small groups were growing independently of the church. These included followers of the Oxford Group Movement or Buchmanites who were receiving a good deal of publicity, some of it adverse. It was to distinguish SCK from such movements that the local units of Servants of Christ the King were not called cells or groups but companies (Lloyd, An Adventure in Discipleship, 1953, p. 44).

There were indeed some superficial similarities between the practices of the Oxford Group Movement and those of the Servants of Christ the King. These similarities even went down to the use of pencils and notepads to write down thoughts in a 'quiet time' and the sharing of these thoughts in a small group. Although some SCK members continued to make notes of thoughts received in the silent time, there was an important difference between SCK and the Oxford Groups in the direction which these thoughts were expected to take. The preparatory work and introduction to the SCK company meeting were designed to focus prayer and thought on a common concern which might become the group's calling to work in the world. SCK members did not meet with the primary aim of advancing their own individual spiritual development, though this was recognised as necessary to the corporate spiritual development of the company. Unlike some other cell groups, this was certainly not a place for regular public confessions. The external focus of prayer and the rules of controlled discussion helped to restrain the possible development of a hothouse atmosphere. The whole SCK method was designed to protect the freedom of each member within the fellowship. Companies were encouraged to be patient, unhurried and unpressured. So greatly did this environment differ from that of a hothouse that twenty years later Olive Parker was complaining that many members never got beyond the pleasantries in their relationships with one another.

> I have sometimes wondered whether this [loss of feeling of adventure and expectancy] comes on companies because they try to stick at the point where a deeper understanding of each other's needs and talents would lead to a breaking-down of their reserve. It can be difficult to balance the restraints of courtesy with the need for honesty within the company bond. Honesty to each other nearly always leads to pain and difficulty but through it comes the joy of fellowship on a deeper level, and the company life is renewed rather than dwindling away. (Parker, An Essay in Self-Examination, 1963, p. 5)

Group processes, which psychologists, anthropologists and others had been studying and writing about for years, were now in the 1960s being discussed more widely in business and society. Many people had become involved in encounter groups, T-groups and other intensive small groups at work, or in therapeutic groups of one kind and another. The processes of any small group, whether intensive or not, were liable to be analysed by both professionals and amateurs. Although some individuals within SCK had received training in this field and wrote occasional articles in the Newsletter (Willis, 1968), they seem to have had little impact on the movement as a whole.

> The whole subject of relationships in groups has been given a great deal of attention in recent years in secular and church circles. We talk about groups and fellowship endlessly. We are even supposed to have a special insight of our own because we wait on God together. Yet we are not willing, much less eager, to avail ourselves of the knowledge that has grown up while we have been comfortably 'doing things the SCK way'. (Parker, Call to Commitment, 1964, p. 8)

A recurring criticism of Christian small groups has been that powerful group dynamics can be in control, rather than the workings of the Holy Spirit. Group members may fail to recognise what is really going on, carried along by naïve optimism and attached to an ideal picture of what the group is supposed to be while acting in ways that can even be directly opposed to that ideal. In the worst case, a charismatic leader aware of these dynamics can use them to manipulate the group to his or her own ends. Training everyone in group dynamics is not a complete answer. A group can spend too much time thinking about itself and not enough working on a real common concern. But the answer is surely not to try to do without small groups altogether. They are inescapably part of church life, not least whenever there are tasks to be done. The question then is not whether to allow small groups within the church – they can hardly be avoided – but how they can be encouraged in their creativity yet restrained by a wider accountability. The requirement for every company to have a priest-adviser was one way in which the founders of SCK tried to guard against delusions and keep groups within the guidance of the church.

Faced with the rise of communism and fascism in the 1930s, Roger Lloyd struggled with the tension between corporate unity and personal freedom. In his books written up to 1937 he took the view that Christians should always take the side of the individual against the community when the two came into conflict. He recanted this view in his book *The*

Beloved Community (Lloyd, The Beloved Community, 1937). Believing humans to be social animals who were unable to escape from community with others, he reluctantly concluded that Christians 'must decline to be communal at the expense of the individual, or individualistic at the expense of the community' (Lloyd, The Beloved Community, 1937, p. 28). The tension between the two was necessary but should be maintained on a fruitful and creative level, 'rooted and grounded in the acceptance of the spiritual interpretation and basis of all life' (Lloyd, The Beloved Community, 1937, p. 30). At that time Roger Lloyd was writing about communities on a national and international scale. But the same idea of fruitful and creative tension between individual and group can be seen in the design of the companies of the Servants of Christ the King.

SCK rule and practice recognised the tension between personal freedom and communal loyalty. Under the rule, members promised to be obedient to decisions of their company, but these decisions could be made only with the agreement of every member. The unanimity rule alone could not guarantee personal freedom, since unanimity in decision-making can be arrived at by processes of groupthink or even outright coercion. But the SCK practice of waiting on God affirmed the value of every contribution to group discussion and was designed to encourage dissenting or uncertain voices to be heard. By prohibiting interruptions, challenges and questioning, 'controlled discussion' gave every member of the group freedom to say things which others might not want to hear. Gonville ffrench-Beytagh wrote about the way in which the communal and the personal could come together in unanimous decision-making:

> [T]he 'unanimous decision' which SCK demands need not be one that each member enthusiastically agrees upon. It may be one which a strong majority agrees upon and with which the others, in love, concur. But if there is one who still, in love, is convicted that the proposed action should not be taken, it cannot in fact be taken. (ffrench-Beytagh, Advice on Waiting upon God, 1972)

The key word here is 'love'. Without love, as well as structure and guidance, SCK companies could – and occasionally did – lose their freedom to the tyranny of one individual unwilling to listen to the others, or to the tyranny of the group unprepared to hear its 'awkward' members. A special kind of leadership was sometimes needed to enable the group to keep listening to and bearing with one another, and to encourage love, patience and honesty. At one time training was offered for company leaders. Later most companies rotated leadership between their members, who were largely without explicit training. This was perhaps a suitable arrangement for well-established groups whose members had already reached a deep fellowship with one another, but it did not always work well in new or ad hoc groups, for example during the annual conference.

Although some SCK companies stayed together for many years and became centres of deep fellowship, leaving a company was always relatively easy. On the other hand joining SCK was quite difficult in the early years when there was a probationary period before full membership. The no-publicity rule made it difficult even to find an SCK company. But once in, there was no obligation to stay. The SCK promise made by members, until it was eventually dropped altogether, was made for one year at a time and not for life. The freedom to leave is in marked contrast with groups which try to control their members. It was never intended that an SCK company would be the only centre of fellowship for its members. Most SCK companies, other than student groups, were originally in Anglican parishes and many remained thus connected even after non-Anglicans were admitted to the movement.

Roger Lloyd wrote in 1953 that from the beginning of SCK the relationship between the company and the parish had always been the greatest difficulty of all (Lloyd, An Adventure in Discipleship, 1953, p. 31). Throughout the life of SCK there have been incumbents who feared that an SCK company might divide their congregation. Although SCK never was nor sought to be a church, there were other movements which had begun within a church and gone on to set up churches of their own. A fellowship within a fellowship can be a blessing or a threat, a group of companions or a clique, even a gang. Does the close fellowship of the small group take away from or contribute to the wider fellowship of the parish, the church, the world? Examples could be quoted in both directions. Here is one from an Anglican parish priest:

> [In my own parish] we have two companies. If you were to ask them what they do, you will probably get the usual answer – 'nothing very much'. Yet I am convinced that they have played a very large part in changing the whole tone of the parish. A few years ago, it was a byword for disunity and stand-offishness. There were factions that would not speak to each other. Newcomers again and again complained that they weren't wanted. The SCK companies set themselves the task of praying for the unity of the parish, and, as a result, a large number of families as well as of individuals have been brought right into the church, because, as they have said, they found such a close family spirit in the congregation that they wanted to be inside. The SCK members

themselves would not claim that they are in any way responsible for the change of spirit, but I am quite sure that they are. I would describe them in words which Olive Parker used in the little booklet *In Company Together*: 'The Servants of Christ the King are ordinary people trying to show that going to Church means that they are really members of a family.'[1] (Rudd, 1960, p. 7)

As in the above example, relationships between the small and the wider group have to be prayed for and worked at. Maintaining these connections is perhaps even more difficult in the twenty-first century, when many people seem to have loose attachments to overlapping or totally unrelated groups with deep commitment to none. Churches have struggled with what seems to be a widespread aversion to church membership even on the part of people who claim to believe in God. Some have seen small groups as a means of bringing non-churchgoers into a Christian fellowship alongside or even in place of the traditional congregation (Archbishops' Council, 2009, pp. 52-7). Although an SCK conference explored the ideas of 'New Way of Being Church' (Smyly, 2006), SCK companies have not attempted to take the place of traditional structures. A survey of SCK members in 2007-8 reported:

> The overwhelming majority of those interviewed were worshipping members of the Anglican church, the exceptions being one Russian Orthodox, one Quaker, one Methodist and three Catholic. ... Although a number of people found difficulty with the kind of worship they now encounter in their parish churches, and some were too disabled to get there, no-one had abandoned institutional religion altogether. (Norman, Snapshot of SCK in 2007-08, 2009, pp. 7-8)

The Christian church has always prayed for and sometimes worked for fellowship and community. There is scope for disagreement about the relative values of small and large, residential and part-time, homogeneous and diverse, rural and urban communities and how all these different types might fit together. But whatever the structures, deep fellowship seems to be essential to the kingdom. Saint Paul wrote repeatedly about Christians as members of Christ's body in which each needs the others (Romans 12:3-8; 1 Corinthians 12:12-17; Ephesians 4:11-16). We are indeed each answerable before God for our actions but, as Saint Augustine said in his sermon on the Eucharist, 'We are not saved alone'.

---

1   The reference is to (SCK, 1960)

In his little book *The Inspiration of God*, published in 1944 and dedicated to Edmund Morgan, Roger Lloyd claimed that to know the inspired life it was necessary to dwell in true community. He applied this principle to the arts as well as to religion. He conceded that to write a symphony you needed to go away into solitariness. But, he asserted, the impulse to create it and the discipline to keep at it could only come from belonging to the appropriate social milieu (Lloyd, The Inspiration of God, 1944, pp. 91-2). In an earlier chapter he posed the question 'how can we be inspired by God?' and tried to answer it by setting out a programme of action. We had to become members of consecrated communities (Lloyd, The Inspiration of God, 1944, pp. 33-4). A parish could be a consecrated community, but so also, alongside or in the parish, could a small cell of convinced lay Christians. Small cells which set out with this aim had to train themselves to respond to the divine initiative so as to become a community capable of receiving God's inspiration for the work they were called to do (Lloyd, The Inspiration of God, 1944, p. 37).

Roger Lloyd's claim was that we were able to '*create for ourselves the mould in which* [God's inspiration] *can best be given and received*' (my emphasis). This could be read as seeking preferential treatment, or trying to constrain and even control the Holy Spirit. Does the Holy Spirit really give priority to community as the place of inspiration? What if inspiration does not seem to come, or at any rate we do not recognise it as having come? Do we blame ourselves or God? These questions began to arise as SCK companies came into being and experienced the reality of waiting on God together. Some of them were picked up by Edmund Morgan when he addressed the SCK conference (Morgan, Waiting upon God: An Explanation, 1944). Whilst accepting the premiss that the Holy Spirit 'works in and through individuals as members, not as unrelated individuals', he insisted that it was the Holy Spirit who was the weaver of fellowship. We could not create the fellowship of the Holy Spirit for ourselves: at most we could offer and allow ourselves to be woven together. God's guidance was readily available, but not necessarily in the form of answers to our questions. It was often long-term guidance which led into relationship. It was readily available if we were ready to hear it:

> We may ... confidently expect the loving guidance of God. It is evidently his desire to give it us. And it is characteristically experienced in fellowship. We are more likely to have come near to what God wants us to see if we have reached a common mind as a company of praying people than if we remain isolated individuals. (Morgan, Waiting upon God: An Explanation, 1944)

CHAPTER TEN

IN COMPANY

The whole existence of the Servants of Christ the King depended on its small groups, known within the movement as companies. Central organisation was intended to be minimal. There were many companies which had little connection with the centre apart from receiving the Newsletter, and there could well have been other groups practising the SCK method without even this connection. What actually took place in companies was not always known to the Warden, Secretary or Central Company, and sometimes it was not what they would have recommended or expected. There was no system of inspection and many companies never invited visitation (Babington, Company News, 1963, p. 17).

The original design for SCK envisaged two types of companies: those based on Church of England parishes and those based on a shared place of work or common expertise (termed 'vocational companies'). In practice, most of the groups which actually came into being were parish-based, the main exceptions being companies of students in colleges and universities. At the beginning, during wartime, there were a few companies in the armed forces. Initially clergy were not allowed to become members of companies, but the rules were changed in 1944 and clergy companies were started. Later, clergy were no longer confined to separate companies, but some clergy companies continued. Another type of company developed when the administration of SCK began to be shared beyond the Cathedral Close at Winchester: groups which took on general responsibilities or particular tasks were constituted with titles such as Central Company, Executive Company, Trustees, Special Company, conducting their business by waiting on God in the usual SCK way. In addition there was a Central Youth Company for a few years in the 1960s. A residential company in London between 1962 and 1969 was described in the previous chapter. A 'Shadow Company' was formed in 1965 consisting of scattered members who undertook to pray for office-holders and others within the movement.

There were three distinct patterns leading to the formation of companies. The first of these was the initiative of local leaders already familiar with SCK, who would invite and encourage individuals or already existing groups to set up or join SCK companies. An open meeting might be held with someone coming from 'central SCK' to give an introductory talk to a whole parish; or specific individuals might be guided into an SCK company by their spiritual director or college chaplain. Some SCK members who went abroad to serve in mission stations took SCK with them. The second way in which companies came into being was as a result of someone reading Roger Lloyd's book *An Adventure in Discipleship* and getting a group of friends or parishioners together to try it out. Some long-lasting companies and future leaders of SCK, including two Wardens and a Secretary, started out in this way. The third pattern of company formation was by cell division. The maximum size of an SCK company was set at twelve and companies whose membership exceeded this number were expected to split. This was practical, in order to allow adequate time for everyone to be heard at meetings, but it also held out hopes of organic growth. However, cell division often turned out to be difficult and it was not uncommon for companies to die soon after they had divided.

Roger Lloyd claimed that deep fellowship was more likely to flourish in groups whose members were similar in age or occupation or homogeneous in some other way (Lloyd, The Inspiration of God, 1944, p. 38). This may have made it easier to bring groups together, but it risked losing sight of an important characteristic of Christ's kingdom, which is open to all sorts and conditions of people. We cannot choose who will sit next to us at the Lord's feast (Luke 14:21-23). As Olive Parker noted, differences of temperament, age and background in the group can help Christians to learn how to be at one with all Christ's people (Parker, The New Commandment, 1962, p. 17). But in reality the SCK way of waiting on God did not immediately appeal to all temperaments, ages and backgrounds. The founders of SCK may have underestimated the discomfort which some people would feel in a group whose practice was based on speaking and listening and where others could seem to be more self-confident, more articulate and more educated than themselves. It was possible to alleviate this discomfort within a caring and sensitive group, given time and good leadership. But, as it turned out, the majority of SCK members had had a university education or some kind of professional training, many were in the caring professions, and few were members of what Roger Lloyd chose to call the 'artisan class' (Norman, Snapshot of SCK in 2007-08, 2009, pp. 2-3).

Although a typical SCK company could hardly be described as a complete cross-section of humanity, there was usually enough diversity to exercise the Christian love and understanding of the group, if the group was prepared to be so exercised. At the deepest level no human group can be completely homogeneous, for each person is unique. There is a tendency for groups to deny diversity in their membership, whether actively by driving out people who are 'different' or, less obviously, by not listening to and learning from the differences and therefore not encouraging these differences to be expressed. The SCK way of waiting on God provided opportunities at every step to express differences, to listen and to learn. Many companies did in fact grow into accepting communities, growing nearer to becoming one in Christ.

Until the mid-1960s every SCK company was expected to have a priest-adviser. The priest-adviser was not the group leader and was not expected to attend every meeting. Some were advisers to more than one SCK company. No doubt practice varied from company to company, but at least in theory the priest-adviser was meant to act as a longstop rather than a director, helping to give pause to hasty decisions and keeping the group anchored within the larger Christian community. Conferences of clergy advisers were held in the early years of SCK (Lloyd, Cancellation of Conference, 1945, p. 2).

Each SCK company appointed its own leader from within its members. At first company leaders were appointed annually (Anon., Waiting upon God, 1945), though in practice some went on for ten years or even more. Training was provided for company leaders up to the 1970s, though there was no definite requirement for leaders to take part in it. Later it became more usual for leadership to be rotated among the members of the group from meeting to meeting, so that the proportion who had had any formal training diminished yet further. Unlike some contemplative prayer groups, SCK did not have a set formula for introducing meetings, so the introduction or 'lead-in' came to depend somewhat on the outlook and personality of the leader. The subsequent stages of the meeting – silence, controlled discussion, open discussion and decision-making – were less dependent on the leader alone and were relatively well defined in the SCK literature which most or all members of the company would have read.

The geographical spread of groups was patchy, as was to be expected in a movement which had started out with no publicity. Out of 109 companies listed in February 1959 no fewer than fifteen were in Ipswich and twenty-three were in the Winchester diocese. More than half of recorded companies throughout the lifetime of SCK were in the southern half of England. Clusters of companies formed in places where someone, usually a clergyman, was active and enthusiastic for SCK: Roger Lloyd and Edmund Morgan in the Winchester diocese, Richard Babington in Ipswich and later Exeter, Ivor Watkins in Bristol, George Willis in Cheltenham. Among the lay members of SCK there were also a few planters of companies, most notably Pauline Haswell (later Stevenson, later Waters) who helped to start companies wherever she went in three continents.

The concentration of companies in a few areas encouraged SCK to move to a measure of regional organisation with each region represented in the Central Company. Some regions held day events at which members from different companies could meet one another. A 1964 report described the regional picture.

> [I]t may be interesting to list the regions with the number of companies in each as accurately as we know it:
>
> London: 20
>
> Winchester: 17
>
> Bristol: 7
>
> East Anglia: 16
>
> Devon and Cornwall: 18
>
> North-west: 14
>
> Scattered Companies: 22
>
> The scattered companies vary from those like Repton, which have been in existence for some years now with very little opportunity of meeting others in SCK, except for the one or two people who can manage the annual conference, to the newest company in Hull which seems to be perpetuating the tradition that there shall always be one lone company in Yorkshire.
>
> There are, so far as we know, twenty companies overseas and the one area where enough companies are in existence to feel themselves on a regional basis is Cape Province. (SCK, 1964)

There was no such thing as a typical SCK company. The practice of waiting on God was the only common factor. This practice could have been learned from reading Roger Lloyd's book *An Adventure in Discipleship* or other publications, from members who had experienced other SCK companies, from participation in group meetings at the annual SCK conference, or in 'taster' sessions arranged by sympathetic clergy.

What were these companies actually led to do? Roger Lloyd described his difficulty in answering this question when it came up, as it often did after he had given one of his talks on SCK to a church group. He felt unable to give the real answer which was 'whatever the Holy Spirit tells them to do', because that would require a further half-hour of explanation. He continued:

> So one is tempted to fall back on the 'success' stories of the really exciting adventures which have happened to one company or another. But this is truly a temptation, and therefore to be resisted. For the companies to whom that kind of thing happens are really very few and one must not suggest that obviously romantic adventures are going to happen to them all. To single out those few just because they offer a story which can be told is to suggest what is obviously false, namely that the worth of a company is to be judged by the wealth of its adventures. (Lloyd, But What Do These Companies Actually Do?, 1957)

Perhaps Roger Lloyd had known this temptation when writing *An Adventure in Discipleship* a few years earlier. Companies which went on steadily from year to year, undertaking humble tasks and allowing themselves to be formed by waiting on God, found it more difficult to write about themselves. Self-reporting by these companies could appear uninspiring, as Gonville ffrench-Beytagh observed at the conference which elected him to be Warden of the movement.

Descriptions of faithful and modest communities are more likely to be found in correspondence rather than in formal reports. We are fortunate in having a letter written in 1947 and addressed to a member of a new company, in which the writer describes her own experience of SCK.

> I think it is a very good idea of yours to want to know about our early beginnings and I will do my very best to tell you all about it, trusting it will be a help. It will be a pleasure for us, for anything to do with SCK I love, whether talking or writing, hearing, or just thinking about it. It is all so wonderful!
>
> ... We had heard about SCK right from the word 'go' because we are fortunate in having Fr. Watkins here in Bristol. He was then the Archdeacon and is now, as you know, the Bishop of Malmesbury. The three of us who started the company know him very well. We belonged

then to a private little fellowship and used to meet regularly for prayer and discussion in a friend's house. There were quite a number of us. The bishop asked if he might come and tell us all about this new idea, hoping, I think, that we would turn our fellowship into a company, or several companies of SCK. We gladly heard all he had to say, and then did nothing about it! But there it was, at the back of our minds, and after about eighteen months, the seed began to spring to life and we three ... got together and made up our minds to start a company. We told the bishop what was in our minds and he kindly invited us to his home, where he spent an evening talking to us and getting the very essence of SCK into our beings. The first thing we had to do was to have a leader and find an adviser. So we three met and prayed together. We were fortunate in having belonged to that other fellowship, so that we were quite used to praying and meditating together. We are all three teachers and belong to a Teachers' Guild, the Guild of the Good Shepherd, and that too was a help, because that is another way of knowing one another intimately. The result of our prayer was that I became the leader and a priest, quite unknown to us before, became our adviser. We soon gathered two more people, and then another one. It took us some time to study the SCK papers to find out just what was expected of us. We couldn't meet more than once a month, because most of us are very busy people and in addition have responsibilities at home. Our first need was to make our Company Rule based on the framework of the General SCK Rule, so we met for several months for that purpose. Each time we met for this waiting upon God, I used to give a short summary of what we should strive to do during the time of silent prayer. That is given in the paper *Waiting upon God: An Explanation*. There are four steps which we are advised to take and which we found most useful. We don't need to do that now, but if any new enquirers turn up, I shall revert to that old method, I think.

It was soon borne in upon us that we could not hope to do a thing in the service of God, until we had taken ourselves in hand and endeavoured to deepen and strengthen our own private spiritual lives. So we set to work upon the study of prayer and explored its many intricate paths to the best of our ability. It seemed that we were led by gradual steps until some of us were doing more in our prayer life than we had ever dreamed possible and we were encouraged so much by the fact that we were all at it, and all experiencing failure, and sometimes success. After well over a year, we discovered that prayer was to be our common concern. ... One thing we did learn, was that we had to be patient. We could not hurry or force things, either during our time of silent prayer or during our discussions.

We went through a period of frustration, when we simply could not get on. We could never come to a unanimous decision in our company, owing to one member who seemed to be just 'outside'. We endured this for a long time and it made us feel very unhappy and thwarted. But the time came, when all the difficulty was removed and this particular member left us. Then we went ahead and have never looked back. It is a very happy fellowship indeed and we love to be together, whether for prayer and discussion, for study, corporate communion, a picnic, an evening at the theatre, or whatever else brings us in contact.

We are coming to Winchester on June 6th for the week-end. We hope to have a day of study and prayer and shall renew our promise then.

I think that you having to do without your leader so soon after starting, will help you and strengthen you considerably. So do cling together and the way will open out before you in a wonderful manner. We are thinking of you and praying for you. ...

Our very best wishes to you, and our advice is keep plodding on – it is well worth it. (An SCK company leader in Bristol, 1947)

More than thirty years later, the leader of another company wrote:

The company has been in existence for well over 20 years and still has two original members. We are very fortunate in having at present the excellent encouragement and advice from Father Mark Dalby. At present we have nine members and four enquirers. We do not come from the 'intelligentsia': Doreen and Queenie are housewives and widows; Helen a priest's widow; Iris a mother and housewife suffering from multiple sclerosis; Shirley mother of two young children; Angela a retired secretary; Doris and Eileen civil servants; Brenda a secretary; Bob a storeman, only partially sighted; Tom an accountant and Bruce a clerical worker. Quite a wide age gap. During the course of the years we have had many 'comings and goings' but only one member has left because of incompatibility.

Our meetings are held fortnightly and conducted in the original SCK form. We usually have intercessions before the silence and controlled discussion. The meeting concludes by saying compline together. The rule of the company is the rule of SCK and in addition we have all committed ourselves to say the Lord's Prayer and to pray for each other at 9 a.m. each morning. We are all convinced that this not only draws us together daily, but that we do gain from the support of each other.

We often meet socially together. The company started as a parish company but now consists of people from other parishes – all Church of England. We have never had to face up to the question of absorbing into the company those from other denominations and so the question of being 'ecumenical' has never occurred. Joint meetings and discussions have been held with a group of Roman Catholics and we have spent weekends with them and visited places of interest together.

Among our concerns and efforts have been the following: collecting stamps for the Wantage Sisters and taking an interest in their missionary efforts; over the last few years we have sent a corporate donation to the Church Army at Christmas; decorating rooms for the elderly; decoration (paint, not flowers) of the Church; parish visiting; holding of house meetings to which enquirers into the Christian faith have been welcomed; held house masses; Father Dalby has conducted quiet afternoons in preparation for Christmas and Easter to which others have been invited – these have always concluded with a house mass. Recently we have supported one of our members through a very nasty court case, and Bob is taking an interest in work with the blind.

Members have attended the SCK conferences and returned to the company refreshed with new ideas.

We are a little concerned when SCK talk about spreading the idea of SCK in the universities and/or hospitals. While we go along with this in theory we feel that perhaps the appeal should be to the ordinary man or woman in the pew who, not having a specialist vocation, needs the support of belonging to a group of Christians. The apostles were not the 'intelligentsia' of their day. The idea of going after the 'higher classes' appears to be the failing of the Church of England! (Knight, 1979)

From the beginning until the 1970s there were SCK companies in colleges around the country. These tended to come and go as one generation of students succeeded another, as described by a university chaplain in 1979:

In the autumn of 1977 the University of Essex chaplaincy's annual retreat at Hengrave Hall, Bury St Edmunds, coincided with a day gathering of members of SCK from East Anglia. As a result we built Canon ffrench-Beytagh into our retreat programme, and enabled the students to learn something of the aims and techniques of SCK. In particular we heard about 'waiting on God' and the concept of SCK 'companies'.

The students wanted to stay together as a group after the retreat, and decided to adopt an informal kind of SCK structure.

For the rest of that academic year, the group, about fifteen in number, met fortnightly on a Sunday afternoon for three hours. The first hour was spent on waiting on God and sharing insights; the second on more general discussion, and the third in 'breaking bread' over tea, to which each person contributed something. (We found ourselves with an embarrassing surplus of food in quite a short time!)

Not every member was able to come to every meeting, and we did not attempt any very demanding discipline. But it was remarkable in the student context how many people did make it a priority, and how there developed very quickly a sense that to be absent was not only to deprive oneself of companionship but to inflict loss on the group. The group was completely ecumenical with Roman Catholics, Anglicans and free church people present, though denominational labels were ignored and forgotten about in the search for a Christian response to each other's insights and offerings.

At the end of the academic year the group dispersed and did not reform. This lack of continuity is a fact that has to be lived with in chaplaincy work. It has the advantage that a University chaplain does not have to live with his mistakes (they leave after three years!), but the corresponding disadvantage that much has to be re-started and re-learned each year. For this reason I doubt whether a chaplaincy has the degree of stability necessary to build and maintain a properly constituted SCK company, but there is no doubt that the meeting to wait upon God, the sharing of insights and the breaking of bread can prove valuable means of helping students to deepen their faith in and commitment to Our Lord Jesus Christ. (Thom, 1979)

Among the SCK people interviewed by Alison Norman in 2007-8 were several members of clergy companies. One of them described what the company had meant to him.

[He] feels it has contributed a great deal to the ministry of its members. In its early days the company had eight to ten members and a strong emphasis on finding and following up a common concern. They were, for example, active in getting a chaplain appointed to [a local hospital] and in developing 'learning for earning' courses which helped young people to acquire social responsibility and make use of job opportunities. Members also sometimes went on trips abroad together. ...

Now the clergy company has only six members and all but one are retired. Like most SCK companies there is no longer an active concern but the pattern of meeting has not changed from its early days. They meet monthly, rotating round different members' homes, and start at 10 a.m. with Communion, followed (with no further introduction) by fifteen minutes silence, controlled discussion, general discussion. There is coffee after the meeting. Deep friendships and mutual trust have been built up. Also personal and parish problems are sometimes raised which could not be shared more widely. 'It has been an oasis – we have quiet together, think together, pray together'. However it seems impossible to attract new, younger members, though they have tried hard. Also there has been no motivation for getting involved with the wider SCK movement and this is seen as an essentially lay organisation.

[He] has tried to get companies going in his parishes but the idea has never got off the ground although the SCK method of meeting has often been used. (Norman, Anthology of SCK members' lives, 2007-08)

Overseas companies were even more diverse than those in England. Many of them were far distant from other SCK companies and were linked with the rest of the movement only by occasional correspondence, or by expatriate priests or missionary workers who travelled back to England from time to time. A donor offered funds to enable someone from central SCK to visit Africa, but the proposal was not considered practicable (SCK Central Company, 1960). There were SCK companies in various parts of Africa, but only those in Cape Province in South Africa were close enough to be in regular touch with one another. There was, as far as is known, only one company in China and of that there is no record beyond 1949. The Church Missionary Society (CMS) worker who had started it went on to Malaya and from there to Hong Kong and attended a number of SCK conferences when on leave in England (SCK, 1958, p. 5). There were a few companies in Australia, New Zealand, Canada and the United States of America (Greasley, 1965). In 1974 the SCK Newsletter carried a letter from the leader of a company in St Vincent in the Caribbean giving a lively picture of the company's life:

Our company started in 1968. I got interested in SCK through reading *The New Commandment* by Olive Parker which was lent to me by our rector, Fr. Harradine. After I had finished it, Fr. Harradine and I discussed SCK and thus it came that we could make a try with SCK in our parish. So six young people gathered at the rectory and decided to form a company. Of the original six, only two remain. The others went overseas and two went to university and are still there.

Of our five present members, M. and I are teachers, J. is going to Junior High School, Miss L. is in her late seventies and was just a domestic servant, and E. takes care of her father and mother. She only went to primary school. All of us are from simple, poor ordinary families. As West Indians, some of us wonder where our next meal is coming from. J., E. and Miss L. became members after attending one of our meetings because of the peace and quietness they found there. Miss L. says: 'All the past years I have been asked to join the Guild of the Sacred Heart of Jesus and other church organisations. I refused because there are always arguments at their meetings. But now I am a member of SCK. There is peace and quietness at its meetings. God is given a chance to speak to me and there is unity at SCK meetings.' Miss L. speaks for my company.

Our concerns are visiting the sick; running a small library for the parish; helping at missions, and intercession.

The sick always find it a blessing when we visit them. We sing, pray and read the bible with them. In their time of sickness they seem as though they have no friends but us. They always look out for us.

At the missions we speak on various topics such as 'Why do I need God', 'God forgives sinners', etc. ... We also advertise or spread the news among people about the missions.

The library is not what we hoped it would have been because only a few people are borrowing books. Most people say that they prefer to read novels and not some of those heavy theological works. I can see with them, because we are a people who are just catching ourselves educationally. So only about forty people borrow books, mostly teachers or high school students.

At the intercession each member offers his/her prayers in turn. After each clause we say 'Lord in your mercy, hear our prayer', and we sum it up in the Lord's Prayer. 'Be still and know that I am God.' We value the quiet time very much. In our daily lives we are so busy but in the quarter of an hour's quiet time we are centred on God and God alone. SCK is a great help to me as a teacher and if God gives me life I shall do all I can to foster SCK principles. (An SCK company leader in St Vincent, 1974)

Some companies continued in existence for many years, perhaps the longest living being Uplyme on the Devon-Dorset border which began in 1948 and went on into the twenty-first century. But many others had a relatively short life. We know little about these, apart from the special case of student companies in colleges and universities. Olive Parker lamented the loss of inspiration which she considered to be responsible for the death of many companies. Were these companies 'failures'? Or had they already served their purpose when they disbanded? This is known to God alone.

CHAPTER ELEVEN

BONDS OF FELLOWSHIP

According to Roger Lloyd, the growth of Christian cells in the 1930s was quite unorganised and spontaneous, and therefore untidy and ragged (Lloyd, The Church of England 1900-1965, 1966, pp. 312-3). SCK was meant to be different. Although each local company would find its own way by waiting on God, SCK was to be a fellowship of fellowships. Roger Lloyd regarded organisation as essential. Without it, he believed, small groups and individual members would grow weary and disheartened; would be tempted to give up because results were taking too long; would need help and not know where to turn for it; and would turn inward on themselves and become self-satisfied. He tried to set up a system in which no company would be able to live in isolation from the others, and in which each would be visited by somebody from the centre (Lloyd, An Adventure in Discipleship, 1953, pp. 125-6). But it was to be minimal organisation, since groups had to be free to be guided by the Holy Spirit.

The formal organisation of SCK consisted initially of a Warden appointed by the Anglican Archbishops of Canterbury and York, a Visitor also appointed by the Archbishops, a part-time paid Secretary, an annual conference and a periodic Newsletter. The statement agreed by the founding conference also envisaged the appointment of Diocesan Wardens. All this might seem rather complex and top-heavy, but in practice the Warden and Secretary did practically all the work in the early years. Later, as the burden on Warden and Secretary became too great, additional structures were set up from time to time, including Central Company, Executive Company, a Sub-Warden and Regional Companies. After 1977, when there was neither an office nor a general secretary, the work of holding SCK together was divided and shared between members with roles such as Enquirers Correspondent, Pastoral Correspondent and Newsletter Editor, reporting to Central Company and the annual conference.

Despite the efforts of those at the centre, many SCK companies seem to have been largely indifferent to any kind of organisation beyond receiving the Newsletter and perhaps attending the annual conference. An article in the February 1952 Newsletter was entitled 'Holding the Companies Together'.

> One of the features of SCK has always been that every effort is made to ensure a high degree of fellowship both within the company and between different companies. To this and other problems that arise from it the conference gave a great deal of its time. It seems clear that more will have to be done to give every company the feeling that it is closely attached to the Central and to all other companies. (SCK, 1952)

The solution adopted at the next conference was to enlarge the Central Company to include members from all or most of the geographical areas where SCK was active. It was hoped that this would bring local knowledge into the centre and encourage local intervisitation. This change strengthened Central Company, which for a time replaced the annual conference as the effective governing body of the movement. But that in turn encouraged many local companies to leave the direction of SCK to the Central Company. As Olive Parker was later to write:

> [T]here are two sorts of people in SCK – those who are really only interested in their own company and what it is doing, are extremely loyal to this commitment, but simply want to be let alone to get on with the job, and those who care desperately about the spread of what SCK stands for throughout the church. ([Parker], Structure of SCK, c. 1966)

After the publication of Roger Lloyd's *An Adventure in Discipleship* some groups started up simply on the basis of reading the book. Although some of these eventually linked up with SCK, others may never have become known to the rest of the movement. Clergy companies rarely became involved in the wider movement, perhaps feeling that it was primarily for lay people. Many people may have kept their distance through fear of becoming over-concerned with administration. Olive Parker expressed her frustration in the SCK Newsletter in 1964:

> The second attitude I would have you examine is widespread among you and exceedingly difficult for me to bear. It goes like this: 'It's lovely to belong to a movement which has no organisation. Let's keep it free and loose. We belong to so many committees and dull things like that ...'

May I state as a fact that the opposite to *good* organisation is not *no* organisation but *bad* organisation. The result of this attitude over the years has been that SCK as an entity has crumbled away until there are only a few uneasy regional meetings and half-hearted attempts of companies to meet others. The annual conference is fun and spiritually uplifting but many come through it year after year without any clearer idea of commitment to the movement as a whole. The Central Company members have grown less and less clear about what are their areas of responsibility. The Executive Company, set up in near despair a year ago to give a bit of detailed praying and thinking and decision to the affairs of the whole, has met with reactions that have varied from polite hostility to lukewarm acceptance. (Parker, Call to Commitment, 1964, p. 7)

Some of the opposition to the central organisation was perhaps not to organisation as such, but to the direction which 'central SCK' was taking. Guy Parsloe, a former member of the Central Company, wrote looking back in 1971:

We spent more and more time examining the present state of SCK, framing plans for its aggrandisement, counting and recounting. It seemed to me that SCK was ceasing to be a means of serving the church and was becoming for most of us an end in itself, in fact a mini-church. (Parsloe, 1971)

There were periodic expressions of unease and feelings of failure in SCK, amounting at times to a 'death-wish'. But these seem to have been mainly from people at the centre of the movement. There was never any question of closing down every local company: it would not have been in the power of the centre, nor would many companies have allowed it. The doubt and self-questioning were about the direction and organisation of SCK.

At times SCK was held together by the inspiration and leadership of some significant individuals. Roger Lloyd not only wrote the greater part of every SCK Newsletter and spoke at every SCK conference: his books and newspaper articles were widely read within and well beyond SCK. He continued to have a strong influence on members and companies after he had ceased to be Warden. Olive Parker, though she was never Warden, provided leadership as well as organisation in the post of Secretary. Gonville ffrench-Beytagh was a nationally-known name when he became Warden and provided a much-needed challenge to the movement, though this did not prevent many local companies from going their own way without much reference to the centre.

The Central Company held an extended meeting in 1974 at which a series of talks was given by George Willis, an Anglican priest, long-standing SCK supporter and Diocesan Missioner with deep experience of small groups. The subject of his third and final talk was 'Hope lies in letting go'. This was in response to what seemed to be the perennial question: 'whether ... SCK had outlived its usefulness as an organisation and we should just leave the individual companies to go their own way.' The discussion which followed was full of uncertainty and questioning:

> This [talk] pushed us into talking about our corporate life, both as a company and as a movement. What did 'leadership' mean to us? Is it really a problem of relationship and communication? What kind of leadership did Jesus give? When we talk about an individual 'leading' a company, or the central company in some sense trying to give a lead to the movement, do we mean a purely administrative role, or a prophetic 'see what I've glimpsed' role or an exemplary 'do what I'm doing' role? And if, as a central company we don't do any of these very effectively, is it our fault? Or does the reason lie in the autonomous structure of SCK, or perhaps in the nature of the world and the Church at this time of tremendous transition, when nothing can be expected to retain its old shape? (Norman, Thirty-Six Hours, 1975, p. 12)

But it was not only organisation and leadership that bound SCK companies together. There was a measure of shared identity: members were bound together by a common rule, a common commitment to the Church of England, and even the name 'The Servants of Christ the King'. In the earliest period there was also, at least in theory, the common 'super-concern' of evangelism.

SCK began as an Order and had what Roger Lloyd described as 'a stiff and difficult devotional rule' (Lloyd, The Inspiration of God, 1944, p. 37) by which members promised to live after completing a probationary period. The rule and promise were retained when SCK no longer regarded itself as an Order. Membership cards for probationers and full members were signed by a diocesan representative and by the priest-adviser. Modifications were made to the rule from time to time. Companies were free to make their own rules which, however, were expected to supplement rather than replace the general SCK rule. The promise was renewed annually by each member who remained committed.

Roger Lloyd wrote an article in 1955 in which he acknowledged the difficulty which some people had with rules of life, but affirmed the importance of the rule for SCK:

[E]very company must have its rule of life. This has been one of the unvarying features of SCK from the very beginning, and no one has ever proposed that companies should do without such a rule. But many people are puzzled by it, and this requirement does put off quite a number of excellent Christian people … (Lloyd, Why SCK Companies Must Have a Rule of Life, 1955, p. 4)

He argued for rules in general on the grounds that 'they save us from being ruled by our feelings, which are always a bad guide'. But for him the SCK or Company Rule had the special property of being an expression of community:

[E]very SCK member tries to be obedient to a corporate rather than an individual rule of life. It is 'the rule of my company' and not 'my own rule of life.' Further, every member has the duty to help to draw it up, and, when it seems necessary, the chance to ask for it to be changed, for no rule is binding in an SCK company unless and until it has been accepted by all freely and unanimously. (Lloyd, Why SCK Companies Must Have a Rule of Life, 1955, pp. 4-5)

He went on to quote the words of Bishop George Hubback, who was at that time the recently appointed Visitor of SCK:

Our companies have rules of life in order that we may live not individual but corporate lives within the Church, which is the body of Christ. … The expression of the divine life is always self-giving, so we keep a rule along with our fellows in order to curb our selfishness and set us free to give, with them, everything we have to offer. (Lloyd, Why SCK Companies Must Have a Rule of Life, 1955, p. 5)

Roger Lloyd concluded:

Individual rules of life are more constantly broken than corporate ones, because with a corporate one we are being obedient to each other as well as to God. … If we are any use to the Church in her mission it is largely because SCK consists of people who are trying to lead the disciplined life, and trying to do it corporately. (Lloyd, Why SCK Companies Must Have a Rule of Life, 1955, p. 6)

Although Roger Lloyd's article placed much emphasis on the autonomy of each company in setting its own rule, the General Rule was the common factor which brought all the local rules together. When Julian Rudd addressed the SCK conference in 1960, the title of his talk, 'The Application of the SCK Rule' (Rudd, 1960), implied that there was a rule for the whole of SCK and the question was how it was to be followed in practice and with what results. There was a whole chapter in Olive Parker's book, published in 1962, entitled 'The General Rule of The Servants of Christ the King' (Parker, The New Commandment, 1962, pp. 67-74).

When SCK opened its membership to non-Anglicans in 1964, it became necessary to reconsider the General Rule, which had hardly changed since 1943. Clearly the commitment to be a faithful member of the Anglican Communion had to go. Even the obligation to receive Holy Communion regularly would not fit well with the practices of some denominations and would exclude Quakers altogether, unless they were in dual membership with another church. Proposals for possible changes to the SCK General Rule ranged widely. Some were in favour of a return to the original idea of an order with a life-long commitment. Others felt that an annual promise was more appropriate for membership of local groups which might form, re-form and disband for a variety of reasons. Discussions continued at the centre of SCK for several years after this, but in practice companies began to go their own way. Alison Norman reported in 1974 that even the Central Company had not renewed its annual promise since 1971. Although she found one company still living by a strict rule and other companies at least re-dedicating themselves annually, there were many people who took a different view:

> [M]any people felt that the promise was divisive, rather than being a focus for unity, because it excluded those who for one reason or another did not feel prepared to make it and yet who might feel a deep need and wish to belong to a company. These include people (among them our Warden!) who feel that making any promise is such a momentous and binding thing that they do so as seldom as possible and would not want to put pressure on anyone else to make one. Then there are those who feel that any further act of commitment detracts from their baptismal promises and their membership of the Church. ... A company of teenagers had also decided not to make the promise because they were nervous of the degree of commitment which they felt was involved. 'It's a bit binding.' 'I want to keep my options open.' 'It sounds too much like the law – I don't want to feel tied – I want to do things because I want to do them, not because I have promised to.' (Norman, Pilgrim's report, 1974, pp. 18-19)

By the turn of the millennium, the SCK promise and rule were all but dead. Austin Thorburn, the Enquirers Correspondent at that time, was almost alone in trying to revive them. In an article entitled 'Is SCK a Movement?' he wrote:

In the early days of SCK a person became a 'member' by joining a company and by making a personal act of commitment to dedicate him- or herself to the SCK objectives, including attending company meetings. Someone has suggested that some form of commitment be again offered to enquirers and members. At our conference the Warden succeeded in keeping this on the agenda for further consideration, but most of those who spoke about this said that 'enquirers don't want to commit themselves to attend meetings regularly'. It was even said that the word 'member' is inappropriate. I disagree. (Austin Thorburn, Is SCK a Movement?, 1998, p. 20)

Austin Thorburn again pleaded for a return to commitment when he gave three talks at the 1999 conference on 'Reflections on the Benedictine Rule'.

If we accept or have accepted a rule to guide our Christian discipleship, at its best it will enable us to discover that the God of the interior journey is the same God we will encounter on our journey outward … I pray that we may find such a rule and through it the integrity of authentic pilgrimage. We shall count ourselves blest if on that pilgrimage we find opportunity by service and by word to share the truth which the Holy Spirit shows us. (Austin Thorburn, Reflections on the Benedictine Rule, 1999, p. 19)

As we have seen, the bonds which held SCK together as a fellowship of fellowships were already loosening in the 1960s and continued to loosen in the succeeding years. The centre had never sought to impose control on local groups, which were regarded as primary. Almost from the beginning there had been groups which owed their beginnings to SCK but maintained little or no contact with the centre. Some chose to call themselves SCK companies but others deliberately refused the name. Some may have existed entirely unknown to the rest of SCK.

Although some companies gave reports at the annual conference, there was never a system of inspection or accountability to the SCK centre. In the original design, companies were made accountable not to the centre of SCK but through the structures of the Anglican church. However, the precise location of that accountability (parish, deanery, diocese) was never properly worked out (Lloyd, An Adventure in Discipleship, 1953, pp. 31-2, 103-4). Accountability through the church was further weakened when SCK membership was opened to non-Anglicans and companies became multi-denominational. Ecumenical bodies such as local Councils of Churches and later Churches Together were generally not strong enough and appear to have had no part in overseeing SCK companies. The SCK General Rule set a standard, maintained not by inspection but by conscientious promise-keeping and peer encouragement. However, when individual self-actualisation became so highly valued in society and even within the church, it became more and more difficult to maintain even a local common rule, let alone a common rule for the movement as a whole.

In the later years, as the membership of SCK became more elderly and more scattered, there were increasing numbers of people who were no longer in a company or never had the opportunity of being in one. What remained of the centre, by now entirely voluntary and unpaid, felt a responsibility for maintaining contact and offering some kind of pastoral care if only by correspondence. The programme of the annual conference had for many years, perhaps always, included some time for breaking into smaller groups to wait on God, and this became the only opportunity for some people to experience waiting on God in the SCK way. Although these needs continued, the centre eventually became unsustainable when there were no longer enough able-bodied people to attend Central Company meetings and undertake organisational responsibilities.

The decision to close the central organisation of SCK was taken at the final conference in 2014. It had already been felt for some years that it was more important for groups to wait on God than to belong to SCK. My booklet *Waiting on God*, published in 2013 (Bridge, Waiting on God, 2013), was mainly concerned with the workings of the Holy Spirit in the local group and accountability through the local church. The benefits of networking with other similar groups were mentioned but not stressed.

SCK would not even have begun without some central organisation. This distinguished SCK from the isolated autonomous Christian cells which were coming into being in the late 1930s. But the central organisation was deliberately limited in its scope and powers over local groups. SCK companies could not be used as instruments in the exercise of central control. The ninth of Lenin's twenty-one conditions for admission to the Communist International called for the setting up of communist cells, adding: 'The communist cells must be completely subordinated to the party as a whole.' (Communist International, 1920) In recent years some cell churches appear to have adopted a similar model. This was not the SCK way.

A committed but limited central organisation had some advantages. Until SCK discarded the principle of no publicity, the main benefits were seen in the prophetic leadership of Roger Lloyd, the training of local leaders, the networking between companies and the assistance given by established companies to those which were just starting. After SCK had decided to go public, the central organisation was able to provide visibility for the movement and its concepts, and to link enquirers into suitable local groups where these existed. However, it is not clear whether or how central SCK could have dealt with companies which went off the rails. This might have been done, for example, by withdrawing the right to use the title 'Servants of Christ the King' if a group was considered to have departed from its Christian basis or to be involved in abusive practices of some kind. But there was never such a withdrawal of accreditation. If intervention was needed, it was more likely to have been made locally by the priest-adviser while priest-advisers existed in SCK, or by the incumbent of the parish, either of whom would have had the power *de facto* to close down the company.

After the retirement of the last paid Secretary in 1967, SCK came to depend entirely on volunteers to organise the conference, edit and send out the Newsletter, commission and send out publicity material, promote regional meetings and retreats, answer correspondence from enquirers and scattered members and generally to maintain the network. Networking can be valuable but begets administration and brings with it the danger of encouraging the 'committee mind' against which Reginald Somerset Ward had warned ([Ward], 1937). SCK Central Company and SCK trustees did indeed resist this temptation, meeting and waiting on God as companies. But an ageing membership was eventually unable to sustain the effort of travelling and administration. Local groups can and do continue to meet and wait on God in the SCK way, but are no longer able to look to a central organisation to sustain networking. The 'fellowship of fellowships' was a distinctive feature of SCK for over seventy years and its passing is a sad necessity.

CHAPTER TWELVE

RUNNING THE COURSE

The Servants of Christ the King never became the powerful force for the Christianisation (indeed the Anglicanisation!) of English society which their founders had envisaged. This aim was impossibly ambitious from the start and was gradually abandoned. Had it remained, it would have faced fresh challenges when Britain began to embrace a wider range of cultures and faiths. Out of this failure came a better understanding of what waiting on God really meant. The aim was now to help participants to be receptive and faithful to a shared God-given vocation. The naturally contemplative would be encouraged to act after contemplating; the naturally activist would be led to contemplate before acting; individualists would be helped to join in loving community; the dominant and extroverted would learn to make space for others to be themselves.

The principle of no publicity meant that seeds sown in 1943 had to grow in the dark for the first ten years or more. Some grew into plants and put down strong roots. The roots might have been shallower if there had been widespread publicity from the start. But the rate at which these plants were proliferating was necessarily slow. God is not impressed by numbers, but the leaders of SCK sometimes became disappointed and anxious. Relatively few church members were forming or joining SCK companies. Those who did join often appeared to lose their enthusiasm or give up altogether after a few years.

By the early 1960s there was a very different attitude to publicity. This went with a new vision of the discipline of waiting on God, which had been regarded as a special vocation for a few ('Christian commandos'!) but was now being put forward as a way of life potentially available to all Christians (Parker, The New Commandment, 1962, pp. 13-20) (Sister Anne Julian CSMV, 2002, p. 6). However, SCK's opening to publicity came at just the time when the public was becoming less receptive to religion and many were leaving the churches. The discipline of SCK was lighter than it had once been, but it was still a discipline. Although SCK had long ceased to call itself an Order, it still had something of the order about it. Vocations to religious orders were declining even faster than church membership. Even the name 'The Servants of Christ the King' became a stumbling block to some. A new member was quoted as saying 'It sounds so ghastly but it is so wonderful' (SCK, 1979).

Roger Lloyd wrote that theological convictions came first and SCK was an attempt to embody them in the context of mid-twentieth century Britain (Lloyd, An Adventure in Discipleship, 1953, p. 23). The theological claims of SCK seem to have been regarded within the movement as largely self-evident. They were stated again and again by the leadership, but there is no record of their having been publicly defended against criticism. The initial reticence and avoidance of publicity gave little chance for arguments to come out into the open. There were certainly arguments to be had. Suspicions of pietism and illuminism (claiming special access to divine knowledge) might have been in the minds of some people, especially clergy, when they first came into contact with SCK. The support of local clergy was recognised as being important for the growth and continuation of companies (Lloyd, An Adventure in Discipleship, 1953, p. 110). Opposition was indeed experienced in many parishes and led to the closing down of SCK companies or failure even to get started. But grounded reasons for this opposition were apparently not recognised. Opposition was commonly put down to fears of losing control, which of course may have been true in some cases. When SCK at last emerged from hiding it was not strong enough to be regarded as a national threat. It is therefore not surprising that there is no evidence of public controversy. Such controversy would not necessarily have been bad for SCK. It might have sharpened awareness of what SCK was really about.

Although SCK was founded on a theology, there were some members who would gladly have set theology aside altogether. Small groups are a fact of life, both within and outside the church. Some exist to carry on a function – council, choir, kitchen, convent – others to promote a cause, others simply because their members enjoy meeting one another. Any group of Christians can surely benefit from an alternation of prayer and discussion, and the pattern of waiting on God developed by SCK provides a structure within which this can take place. Anyone who has taken part in a Christian committee should be able to recognise the dangers of 'the committee mind' ([Ward], 1937) (Lloyd, An Adventure in Discipleship, 1953, p. 122).

More controversially, some have suggested that the pattern of SCK company meetings could be adapted to groups which were not explicitly Christ-centred, or could be recognised as already existing in, for example, some models of group therapy (Stevenson, 2000). Even in a group not regarding itself as being engaged in waiting on God, these processes might be said to require gifts which a Christian could recognise as gifts of the Holy Spirit: stillness, attentive listening, unforced unity, combination of personal freedom with group solidarity, flexibility, 'being before doing'. Would this be a watering-down or a recovery of essentials, a new vision or a loss of vision? Similar questions are being asked by Buddhists about the appropriation of 'mindfulness' into the secular world. Is this discipline 'ours'? Does it lose its soul if others adapt it to their use?

At various times in its history, SCK looked around for partners and later for successors. They were not found. Although precedents and parallels could be found for every part of their theology and practice, the Servants of Christ the King were unique in the way in which these elements were brought together and related to one another – activity and contemplation, expectancy and flexibility, prayer and discussion, close fellowship and personal freedom. But this was a demanding vocation which went against many of the current trends in the church and in the world. Every time the movement encountered disappointment – failure to grow, apparent failure to make a difference in difficult situations, failure to pass on the vision – there was self-questioning and doubt: the so-called 'SCK death-wish'. Was the SCK vision really God-given? Was it for the many or was it too difficult for any but the few?

Now the course has been run, the story has been told. This book is a record of what we have known and experienced in the Servants of Christ the King. Nothing is now 'ours'. We have received many blessings. The keys of the treasury are in your hands.

PART III

DOCUMENTS

DOCUMENT A

WAITING UPON GOD

Issued to SCK companies as a leaflet 'for private circulation only and not for publication' in 1945, this was a revised and expanded version of a 1943 leaflet with the same title. The author's name is not given, though it may well have been written by Roger Lloyd himself. (Anon., Waiting upon God, 1945)

I.

The Servants of Christ the King was founded in January 1943, with the purpose of offering to God small communities or companies of Anglican communicants, bound together in a common fellowship, leading an ordinary life in the everyday world, and of asking God to make them usable and to use them as he wishes.

This is our aim. In order to bring this aim to pass, the fellowship-life of the company must be fed by corporately waiting for and receiving the divine inspiration and energy. This we call 'waiting upon God'. In one form or another, this activity of a corporate waiting upon the movement of the Holy Spirit has always been a vital part of the life of the divine society: in fact the vigour and health of the church rises and falls in close relationship to the vitality of her corporate prayer. This is what we should expect when we remember our Lord's words, 'Where two or three are gathered together in my name, there am I in the midst of them.' Throughout the New Testament, the association together of Christian disciples in prayer for the descent of the Holy Spirit is taken for granted; and this corporate waiting was the condition of the first Pentecost, and is always the condition of its renewal.

If the companies of the Servants of Christ the King are to carry out their purpose, the vital spirit of each company must be nourished by corporately listening and responding to the demands and the energy of God. And there is no substitute, no short cut. If the Holy Spirit is the Spirit of fellowship, then somehow or other we must get together to receive his inspiration and his enabling. His power comes upon our common friendship, and our companies draw all their vitality from their obedience to this divine order of things. If we are to be used to serve the high purpose of the growth and the expansion of the dominion of Christ over the post-war world – the sole condition of its being a better and a happier world – this being together with God is where we must always start, and where we must be always returning.

This adventure of spiritual fellowship, of intimacy in Christ, of a corporate loyalty to each other in obedience to the Spirit, is the special contribution of the Servants of Christ the King to the church. Corporate waiting upon God in a real interaction of expectancy and receiving is of its very essence. By the unanimous decision of the first conference of the Servants of Christ the King, in January 1943, renewed at the third conference in April 1945, the periodic use of the corporate form of devotion known as 'waiting upon God' is an absolute obligation laid upon every company. As we have a common concern or purpose which all our companies serve, so we must have a common way of seeking the divine power to serve it.

This waiting upon God, however we do it, really reflects a basic attitude to life, and comes out of what we believe to be true about God and man and life. In working out how a particular company of the Servants of Christ the King may best do it, four fundamentals have to be brought together in harmony and balance:

a)   God's initiating energy, showing itself most commonly in his inspiration;

b)   God's Word, the Holy Scriptures, into which his timeless inspiration has been poured;

c)   our human power of reason, which God gave us and means us to use;

d)   our fellowship, or 'togetherness'.

We are too apt to think of waiting upon God as being only a means of discovering God's will in regard to this or that problem on which the company wants to come to the right decision. This use of the phrase is indeed found in the Holy Scriptures, but there are at least four others:

a) the cure of spiritual staleness and the recovery of strength. 'They that wait upon the Lord shall renew their strength';

b) the sense in Psalm 62 of waiting in the stillness for God's deliverance from trouble, where it is equivalent to hope;

c) waiting for enlightenment, for teaching, as the disciples sat at the feet of Jesus;

d) waiting for an expected event, as the apostles before Pentecost, or as anybody might wait in stillness before confirmation or ordination.

II.

The two essential acts in the practice of waiting upon God are silent corporate prayer, and discussion.

Before a company can grow sufficiently in fellowship to be able to decide what kind of work it must do and what witness it must give, its members must learn how to pray and meditate together. A good way of doing this is to choose some subject from the bible for corporate study (for example, the church as the body of Christ), and to select from the bible some passage about the chosen subject, which each member should have read before the meeting. Then, after an opening prayer and a period of silent prayer, each member may be asked to give his interpretation of the passage. The leader should then sum up the opinions of the members, and the company ends the devotion with silent prayer together. We should all experiment in this way with different methods of alternating prayer and discussion together, so that when the time comes to make important decisions, the company may be fully practised in the use of this instrument for the offering of itself for the service of God.

At first a company may, and almost certainly will, have difficulties in using it. But every company has an adviser. Ask him to help. In any case, the constitution of the Servants of Christ the King lays it down that the adviser must approve all unanimous decisions about the kind of action which the company proposes to take. To wait upon God together is like everything else in life: it has to be learned and practised, and the right time to learn it is before the company has been long enough in existence to know what is the purpose God has for it. The normal way of learning it is through corporate meditation upon the bible.

III.

Within the framework of alternating prayer and discussion which is the heart of waiting upon God, every company has complete freedom to experiment, and it should always remember that the bible assigns several meanings, and not only one, to the phrase. But the following way of doing it has been found helpful by many companies, and is the result of a good deal of experience.

We begin with a period of silent prayer. Ten minutes or a quarter of an hour is enough to start with, and it can be increased as the company becomes more practised in the art of praying together in silence. Suggestions about how to spend this time of silent prayer will be found in the leaflet *Waiting upon God: An Explanation*, which we publish as a companion to this leaflet. During this time, everyone sits or kneels, just as he prefers. The leader brings this period to an end by the saying of a prayer or collect.

Then follows the discussion. It is, of course, a discussion not only about the problem itself (if there is a problem: waiting upon God is not solely concerned with the solving of problems), but about the problem or the subject of prayer as interpreted by the common experience of praying together about it. We do not want to discuss the problem academically, but to find out what the Holy Spirit is saying about it to us, as a fellowship.

The discussion is at first controlled. That is, every member is encouraged one by one to give his opinion. The ideas and suggestions thus put forward are not thought of as proposals to be defended, but as contributions to be sifted by the company. So nobody must mind in the least if his particular contribution is rejected; and everybody must speak his mind in unfettered freedom. No offence is given, and none is taken. Nor must anybody mind if his contribution is simply to say that he has no ideas on the subject, or that, as often happens, an earlier speaker has already said what he wanted to say. It is far better to be content to have nothing to say than to misuse the time of prayer in a desperate struggle to find something to say.

Many companies prefer to omit the controlled discussion at first; and certainly it ought not to be undertaken until all the members are convinced that they ought to try. But experience has shown incontestably that the controlled discussion in waiting upon God has a real and deep value. The naturally talkative are restrained and the naturally dumb are encouraged by it; and it is a sacrament of the equality in the Spirit of all the members of the company.

The discussion then becomes free, informal and conversational. It ranges round the suggestions made, but does not yet try to come to a decision about them. This should last for a fixed time – perhaps an hour for the two parts of the discussion. Throughout, the leader must watch carefully for any points, however small, or even negative, on which there seems to be a measure of agreement. At first it will very likely be no more than the sharing of a common perplexity, but later it may become a point of positive agreement.

This point of general agreement becomes the theme of the next period of silent prayer; after it there is again discussion and an attempt is made to record in writing the result of the evening's work. Try to set down on paper any point of unanimous agreement, however slight it may seem to be. But here, as always, nothing is held to be accepted unless the agreement is unanimous. A final prayer by the leader, in which the record is formally offered to God, closes the meeting. It should last about two hours, and once a timetable for it has been fixed, it is important to stick to it.

It may sometimes happen that no unanimous conclusion emerges from the prayer and discussion. But do not let this disturb you. Above all, do not try to force a conclusion when there clearly is none. The real purpose for which the company has met is to offer itself for God's pleasure and the teaching of the Holy Spirit. God will give the members the conclusions that he wants when he sees that the company is ready for them. We spoil everything if we try to force the pace.

This description of what waiting upon God is does not fully cover the ground. The leaflet called *Waiting upon God: An Explanation* is intended to be a supplement to this leaflet, and the two should be read and studied side by side. This other leaflet carefully explains the theology behind it, it warns us of some of the dangers lurking in this path, and it makes some suggestions about how the time of silent prayer may most fruitfully be spent.

IV.

Thus, by waiting upon God, a company renews its strength, receives its life, solves its internal problems, and arrives at a decision about what its work for the kingdom of God is, and how it is to try to do it. But we must be very patient. It will all take time. Probably we shall need a good many such meetings before we can grow together to the point where the company should embark on a programme of action. But when in the end we have come to a unanimous decision we must be loyal to it in the belief that God has guided us to it. In obeying such a decision, we obey him. In the meantime, the patient use of this way of corporate prayer and discussion will nurture more surely than anything else can the growth of true fellowship and true community in the company. There is nothing we are or we do which it does not enrich.

WAITING UPON GOD:
AN EXPLANATION

This leaflet was based on an address given by Edmund Morgan at the
second conference of SCK, held in January 1944. (Morgan, Waiting upon
God: An Explanation, 1944)

The purpose of this paper is to serve as a supplement to the paper already
published under the title *Waiting upon God* in order to give further help
to companies, some of whom have found it a strange and bewildering
exercise.

Waiting upon God is to be regarded not merely as a method or
technique, but as an attitude or temper or mind involving a whole-
hearted desire to learn God's will both for ourselves and for the world, and
consequently a willingness to be convicted by the Spirit of the sin which
blinds us to God's will and thwarts it, and a lively faith in God's desire
to show us his will. It is an attitude of mind grounded in a reasonable
theology and carrying with it certain disciplines – many of them
unexpected – which we shall find to be characteristic disciplines of SCK.

i)   God is creative energy, ever making, ever seeking what he has
      made, ever drawing what he has made to himself. This is an
      activity within the Godhead altogether prior to our response –
      the Father ever giving the Son, the Son ever offering himself to
      the Father, the Holy Spirit ever active in desire that the Father's
      purpose be fulfilled through the Son.

ii)   This creative energy of God is not something which he keeps
      to himself, but is offered to us, and is here and now available to
      all those who in baptism have been made members of Christ,
      the children of God, and inheritors of the kingdom of heaven.

The energy is here, eager to break in upon us. We are inclined to regard ourselves as intelligible, concrete, eager beings, and to regard God's activity as something far off and vague, about which we know next to nothing. We must try to realise the exact opposite. God is eager to break in with power of a very definite kind upon us, but finds us sluggish, double-minded, and slow to respond.

iii) For all this eagerness of the divine desire to break in with power, he waits upon our response. So courteous is he that as he waited upon the Blessed Virgin's 'Behold the handmaid of the Lord; be it unto me according to thy word', so he waits for the same acceptance from us.

This means that it is ours not so much to do things for God, as to fit ourselves to be the kind of people in whom and through whom God can do things.

From this theological background spring directly certain practical disciplines:

a) We shall learn to wait upon God through looking at him together in worship and adoration, and through meditating together, thus allowing God to create the fellowship of the company. Our primary activity is Godward.

b) As we lay ourselves open as a company to this creative energy we must recognise that it is a fearful thing to fall into the hands of the living God. God is terrible not because he is a tyrant, but because he is love. We must be ready to make the venture of faith and to accept the consequences.

c) We shall inevitably be convicted of sin, and find ourselves crying with St Peter: 'Depart from me, for I am a sinful man, O Lord.'

d) If we are obedient in waiting upon God, maybe for a long time nothing seems to happen. If we are not prepared for this it may give us a sense of great frustration. Inasmuch as the authentic energy of God is always veiled, and the veil is the seeming powerlessness of the Cross, every company must expect to pass through the stage of seeming futility. We have to remember that results are God's business, not ours.

Every company must be strong in desire rather than full of ideas. We must be very patient and persevering.

e)   There are times when the opposite happens. We want to hang
      back and God drives us on. Therefore we must be ready to be
      driven forward far further than it is pleasant to go.

This divine energy works in us by the operation of the Holy Spirit who is
given to us in our baptism and confirmation. He works in and through
individuals as members, not as unrelated individuals.

Most people realise that the fellowship of the Spirit refers not
primarily to the work of the Holy Spirit with us and in us as
individuals, but to the bond and relationship which he creates among
Christians. The fellowship of the Spirit is another way of describing
the organic life which we call the church. Yet most Christians are more
conscious of their personal relationship to Christ than of the fact that
this relationship is experienced in fellowship with other disciples.
Failure to show forth the fellowship is perhaps the greatest hindrance
to the gospel in the world to-day. (L. W. Brown, East and West Review,
January 1944)

The Holy Spirit works as a weaver during the fellowship of silence, and if
it be his will, we discover the pattern during discussion afterwards. This
theological fact again determines the character of certain disciplines:

a)   We must learn to speak the truth in love, and be quite frank with
      each other in an atmosphere of sincere friendship. Ideas and
      suggestions put forward in discussion are not to be regarded as
      proposals to be defended, but as contributions to be sifted by the
      fellowship. We do not come with an axe to grind.

      There can be nothing possessive in the life of a company and we
      must be careful about the leadership principle at this point.

b)   The fellowship of the Spirit demands of us loyalty to the company
      and to each other as members of the company. A practical
      expression of this will be found in our making attendance at
      meetings of the company a first claim upon our time.

c)   Our life as a company must not be isolated from the life of regular
      churchmanship on the one side or from our personal spiritual
      life on the other. The discipline of the life of the company puts
      not less but more responsibility upon us faithfully to observe the
      General Rule of the Servants of Christ the King as it applies both
      to regular corporate worship and to an individual rule of life.

The Common Concern

The true being of a company is to live, to receive its life from God, to offer its life for God's use, leaving it to God to choose the form in which that life shall be apparent. But experience shows that no company can continue to offer its life to God in this way unless it is bound together by a common concern. What creates a company is some anxiety which is shared by those who look like becoming a company. They find that they are praying the same sort of prayers about the need of the world. A tentative definition is that the common concern of a company is the reflection of that bit of God's love for the world which is drawing a company together.

Individuals desiring to become a company may know beforehand what their common concern is. Or they may have to discover it after the company is formed. Once we are fully agreed as a company as to what the common concern is we must stick to that concern unless and until the Spirit makes it unmistakeably clear to all the members that he means us to be concerned about something else.

The common concern may be for a group of people in special need, or it may be for a cause. It should not be so wide as to be vague or so local that if we moved it would die out.

How to spend the time in the Fellowship of Silent Prayer

a) We must each stir up the gift of the Spirit which is in us through the laying-on of hands (2 Timothy 1:6), either using our own words or a collect.

b) We must pray for each of the other members present with us that we may be woven into a fellowship by the Spirit and be conscious of ourselves as a company and not as so many isolated individuals.

c) We must offer the company as a fellowship to God, holding it up for him to use, as an offering well-pleasing to God through Jesus Christ. This may grow by God's grace into an act of worship and adoration.

d) We must then pray directly for light and help about the agreed subject for prayer. Meditation on a passage of Scripture may well come in at this point. The ideas which come may seem irrelevant, but they may be seen to fit into the pattern when the time for discussion comes. If no ideas come do not be disturbed.

e) In the ordered discussion which follows the quiet time, every member, starting with the leader, making a short contribution in turn, let everything be put into the melting-pot, however irrelevant it may seem to be.

Guidance

God is Light and in him is no darkness at all. He is Truth and the Spirit leads us into all the Truth. The Good Shepherd leads us onward and leads us home.

We may therefore confidently expect the loving guidance of God. It is evidently his desire to give it us. And it is characteristically experienced in fellowship. We are more likely to have come near to what God wants us to see if we have reached a common mind as a company of praying people than if we remain isolated individuals.

But of course we must never claim infallible guidance. The divine light of truth is inevitably refracted by sin. Our experience of God may be real and first-hand, but it is always entangled with the rest of our experience. Therefore there must always be penitence, self-distrust, and willingness to own our liability to err. 'Not every spirit is of God.'

We must be most carefully on our guard against a mechanical view of prayer and guidance. Some safeguards against this attitude are suggested:

a)   Be rich in thanksgiving, worship, adoration.

b)   It is vastly more important to learn to be the kind of people God can guide than to 'get guidance'.

c)   There is no direct prayer for guidance in the Lord's Prayer, but it is rich in desire.

d)   Let us train ourselves to believe in long-distance guidance, not too easily associating a particular bit of guidance with the prayer immediately preceding it.

e)   Even unanimous decisions of the company are of course fallible and may need to be re-examined, modified, or scrapped in favour of something which seems more likely to be true.

ADVICE ON WAITING UPON GOD

This was written by Gonville ffrench-Beytagh and issued as a leaflet in 1972, the first year of his wardenship of SCK. *(ffrench-Beytagh, Advice on Waiting upon God, 1972)*

I am wholly convinced that the essence and dynamic of SCK lies in the process which we know as 'waiting upon God' – the whole process of the half-hour's silence, followed by the 'controlled discussion', then by open discussion and finally by decision for action, in which each committed member of the company must be agreed. Unless a group practises this process on each and every occasion on which it meets for action (as apart from purely social occasions) it is not, in fact, a company of SCK.

No one, however great an authority he may be on prayer (and I certainly am not one), can lay down rules for this process of 'waiting upon God' or point to a detailed technique. It differs from most forms of corporate prayer and meditation in that it does not exist only for our own spiritual advancement but is designed to explode into action. (Perhaps the Quaker methods are the closest parallel). This 'explosion' may well not be spectacular, because we are 'servants' and servants are not usually called upon to do spectacular things. Most of their work is done behind the scenes and it is done as a matter of obedience. The same applies to us. I have read and learned in discussion with others what I can of this whole process of 'waiting upon God' and I pass on to you what I hope may be useful of what I have learned. I am not particularly enamoured of the phrase 'waiting upon God' (although I do not know a better one). It smacks a little of passivity. Our 'waiting' must not be passive. It is to be an active one, expectant and attentive in which we are actively making ourselves available to God for what he may call upon us to do. After all, the best waiters in hotels and so on are those who are most willing and attentive to those upon whom they are waiting.

Prayer is an intensely personal activity. It is the language of love. It is loving and being loved – an interchange of love between God and me, sometimes flowing strongly and easily; often, on my part, seeming, but only seeming, to dry up. Sometimes it flows from a full heart, and sometimes from an empty, frightened, fearful and frustrated heart. But it is personal and each person prays in his own way. The basis of the prayer life of an SCK company lies in the prayer life of the individual members of that company. Then when the company gathers for its corporate prayer of waiting upon God there is the added power and presence of *koinonia*, the presence of the Spirit of the Lord God, and of Jesus who is the King of whom we are the servants – 'where two or three are gathered together in my name, there am I'.

But corporate prayer does not only flow between God and myself – it flows between us who are brothers in Christ. So in the company silence we commit ourselves to each other as well as to God. We empty ourselves as best we can of everything that militates against mutual love and trust. We reconcile ourselves to each other in the silence. We purposefully set out to love each other and to commit ourselves to each other as well as to him.

The background to, and basis of, any real practice of prayer is self-discipline. If I am a distracted, frenetic person in my daily life I will be the same in my prayer. I do not become a different person when I set out to pray – although I will become so through a long practice of strong, quiet prayer. Therefore the kind of life I lead, the things I do, the books I read all affect my prayer. I must be disciplined about these things if my prayer is ever to be real and dynamic – a source of power. So it all really depends on me. God will play his part without fail. One of the great advantages of corporate silent prayer as we practise it in SCK is that when one member's prayer is weak and distracted it does not really matter, so long as he does not just acquiesce in it. He is carried by the corporate strength of the company as a whole, however small that company may be.

So that, if an SCK company is going to explode into action under the direction of the Lord the Spirit, the first condition is that each person must be a person who prays or is willing to learn to pray in his daily life, and who is accustomed to waiting upon God day by day. He will have to develop his own 'technique', his own manner of doing this. I suggest that each member of SCK should really 'read, mark, learn and inwardly digest' the following books. I do not suggest that they should be studied in company meetings but that each person should read them and take out of each one the things that he thinks can be useful to him as an individual in building up his own 'way' of prayer.

> *School for Prayer* and *Living Prayer* by Archbishop Anthony Bloom (Darton, Longman & Todd)
>
> *Prayer in the Secular City* by Douglas Rhymes (Lutterworth Press)
>
> *Journey Inwards* by F. C. Happold (Darton, Longman & Todd)
>
> *Prayer* by Abhishikta Nanda (SPCK)
>
> *Did you Receive the Spirit?* by Simon Tugwell OP (Darton, Longman & Todd)

All but the last are paperbacks and relatively cheap, and can be passed around. Together with them you should read previous SCK literature on 'waiting upon God' – particularly *Waiting upon God: An Explanation* by Olive Wyon[1] – now out of print but probably to be found somewhere in the company files. But since that was written we have learned much of the traditions and practices of Eastern prayer which can be of value to us and two of the books I have recommended have particular reference to these to add to our own Christian tradition. The practice, for instance, of deliberately breathing deeply to obtain a sense of recollection. Ten deep breaths, each perhaps accompanied by the word 'Jesus' in the heart is one of them. Or of accompanying each deep breath with a recollection of the Holy Spirit whom Jesus breathed upon his disciples. Or of making this deep breathing an act of union with the whole creation which is alive with the breath of God, or of our union with mankind – all these things can accompany the simple act of breathing if we deliberately set out to make it so. These breaths are not 'gasps' but deep breaths from deep down within us – to put it practically and basically, drawn from our stomachs rather than from our lungs.

We cannot be unaware of the charismatic renewal that has been taking place recently in all the main-line churches, and we need to know what is really going on, to read books, to go to groups or meetings and hear speakers on this subject. The Fountain Trust, Central Hall, Durnsford

---

[1] The publication referred to appears to be the booklet by Edmund Morgan which is reproduced as Document B in Part III (Morgan, *Waiting upon God: An Explanation*, 1944). Olive Wyon (1881-1966) was a speaker at the 1958 SCK conference and wrote about SCK in her book on new religious communities (Wyon, 1963, pp. 121-3).

Road, SW19, holds meetings about once a month in London, has a large stock of literature and can put you in touch with any groups that are near to where you live. The reality of the Pentecostal movement is not only speaking in tongues, but fullness of life in the Holy Spirit, openness to the power of the Spirit and the exercise of all the gifts of the Spirit. Those of you who speak in tongues will probably wish to spend some of the half-hour waiting upon God in this way, praying in tongues, inaudibly of course, which is one of the gifts of prayer.

The posture, too, of prayer can be made to be important. In our private prayer we can stand, or sit or kneel. We can do various things with our hands, stretch them out in acts of oblation, self-surrender, acceptance or sacrifice, lift them in praise and thanksgiving, or clasp them together in petition and in love. All these are probably not possible in company meetings – but they can be made in the imagination. In company meetings the posture is normally that of sitting in a circle or half-circle, but we should sit attentively, not uncomfortably, but expectantly, alive, awake to him who is in our midst.

I think that some of the 'technique' or 'mystique' of the SCK manner of waiting upon God can be covered by two sayings of Our Lord. He told us to 'watch and pray'. We are the Servants of Christ the King so we have to watch for his signs and signals, for what he may say to us at any time. We have to watch the local newspaper and the local community to see what its needs are and what needs we may be called upon to fulfil. We have to watch those around us in our families and at our work for the same purpose. Then we have to bring these needs, which may possibly become company concerns, to Our Lord at our company meetings in silent prayer, so that we may have the guidance of the Holy Spirit concerning them. Then, secondly, Jesus said 'not everyone that saith unto me Lord, Lord, shall enter into the kingdom, but he that doeth the will of my Father'. So from the prayer comes the concern and the consequent action. We cannot do everything. We are not meant to. But often where we cannot act ourselves we can bring the need to the notice of those who can, and probably should, take action – the local authority, the welfare agencies or whoever its concern should properly be.

How then does a company wait upon God? In the first instance it takes into serious consideration all that I and others have written about it. That is the background both individually and corporately. Then when the members of the company gather together the meeting begins with the silence, and it begins punctually. If people come from some distance and need a cup of coffee, they should arrive early for this. I myself prefer to have coffee afterwards because I like to feel that the first thing that we do together is to wait upon God – and I prefer coffee when we relax together afterwards – but all this must be worked out by each company. The silence might well formally begin, and begin punctually, by saying together some hymn to the Spirit such as 'Come down O Love Divine' or the verse that begins 'Drop Thy still dews of quietness' (from the hymn 'Dear Lord and Father of Mankind'). Some of the authorities say that it is best to have some symbol which speaks to us of God and upon which we can concentrate our attention. This may be a text, or a word which we have chosen for ourselves or one suggested by the leader. It might be a flower, a crucifix, a glass, a candle, an ikon, a picture – anything under the sun because all things speak of God – and for each member of the company to use or not to use as he likes. But obviously these things and a thousand others have different emotive (or motivating) effects upon us all. What I am asking is that each company should not be afraid to reach out, to experiment, to continue to seek and often to change the symbols which it may, or may not, choose to use in helping its members to concentrate and so to 'wait' upon God. So the silence begins and it may well begin for each one of us with joy – with silent rejoicing, thanksgiving, praise and love – all this as part of emptying ourselves so that we can go on to offering ourselves to him, making ourselves available to him. I suggest that the Jesus Prayer – the words 'Lord Jesus Christ, Son of God, have mercy on me a sinner' might well be used silently by each of us. It can be said over and over again, not as a 'vain repetition' but reflectively, slowly and meditatively. These words can be said with love and thanksgiving as well as in petition and penitence. Others will prefer a text from the bible – 'God is Love' – 'Let us love one another' – or any affective and effective phrase which we can turn over and over in our minds and hearts. But do not try just to do nothing: just resting upon God in quietness is not doing nothing – it is a positive thing in itself. Nor is it any use getting frenetic and battering at God for an answer. We are waiting upon him; but not just waiting – we are leaning towards him feeling out and stretching out towards him, not frantically in desperation, but longingly in love.

During the attempt to do this there are many distractions. What I do about these myself is to have a pencil and paper handy – not particularly to write down any bright ideas – although that is useful in the company silence so that these ideas can be conveyed to the company in the 'controlled discussion'. But I use them to write down my distractions – and my prayer paper normally contains such things as 'Buy petrol – write to Mrs So-and-so' and things like that. If these things come to me in the silence they may well be part of what God intends to say to me –

particularly the letter. But in any event it is no good saying 'I shouldn't be thinking about petrol' and adding to myself 'But I mustn't forget the petrol'. I just write down 'petrol' and then I get on with my prayer and in fact get the best, as it were, of both worlds! Anyway, during this half-hour I must do my best to press towards God not urgently, but strongly and gently, and not to relapse into anger with myself and frustration when I fail. I might use all sorts of words and phrases turning them over in my mind – acceptance, obedience, love, union, availability, wholeness, healing, glory, wonder, power ... any tool or clue that comes to mind – and consider them one by one. All that I emphasise is that during the silence I commit myself to him for whatever he wants. But I must never forget that I must commit myself to my brothers also – it is necessary that 'he who loveth God, love his brother also'. I commit myself to those who are sitting with me in the company. I go mentally around each one and make a silent oblation of myself to him or her, make an act of love towards him, accept him as he is and pray that he may too accept me as I am. It seems to me that at least twenty minutes of the half-hour's silence should be spent on doing all of this.

There are many who would differ and claim, very possibly rightly, that the whole of the half-hour should be spent in this way, of concern with God alone, and that we should not bring in the 'concerns' of the company into this part of waiting upon God but leave them entirely to the 'controlled discussion' when he to whom we have committed ourselves in the silence will guide us. Each company may well practise each method and then consider which they find most fruitful.

But some will say that during the last ten minutes of the silence I may bring before God the one practical company concern. I can ask him to point me and send me where he will, to instruct me with his wisdom as to what needs to be done. Particularly perhaps I might ask him to point out to me those causes and concerns which I in my blindness cannot see for myself. Probably I shall make some notes of all these things, indeed it is important to do so however trivial they may seem. Something that seems trivial may often strike a spark from some other member of the company who has been groping in the same area. We need to remember that we owe it to the company to share what we think we have seen or heard in the silence, unless it is something of a purely personal and private nature which sometimes it may well be.

And so this brings me to the 'controlled discussion'. I cannot too forcibly say that this is an integral part of the process of 'waiting upon God'. Its method is that each person in turn and without interruption contributes to the company what he has seen or heard in the silence –

however trivial or unrelated it may seem to be to the company's present concern. It is the duty of each member of the company to listen, and to listen hard, to what each one has to say. It very often has, and should have, a bearing on what he himself has seen or heard though it is often difficult to detect the connecting link. I must again stress the responsibility of each member to make such a contribution. It obviously cannot be compulsory because the Spirit can move us to silence as well as to speech. A failure to contribute can sometimes be a failure of love and trust, not by the person concerned (we vary very much in our ability to articulate) but on the part of the company as a whole. Where love and trust are growing strongly, shyness must eventually give way to confidence that whatever one says and however badly, it will be welcomed and acceptable. The contribution that each person makes to the 'controlled discussion' should not be a commentary on a previous member's contribution; that comes during the 'open discussion' later on. The contribution to 'controlled discussion' should emerge directly from what one has seen or heard or felt during the silence. It may have no 'practical' implication at all. It may simply be an expression of an awareness of thanksgiving or fellowship or peace – and on the other hand it may well be one also of conviction of a need that the company must seek to fulfil. It is the duty of the leader, and indeed of each member, during the 'controlled discussion' to make notes of those contributions which need further elucidation, consideration, action and so on. One of the reasons for the probationary year in SCK is that probationary members who have not yet committed themselves to God in this particular company may during that year not feel so greatly the responsibility of contributing to the 'controlled discussion' although of course they are completely free to do so. Nor incidentally should their consent be vitally necessary to a company's 'unanimous decision'. And also incidentally the 'unanimous decision' which SCK demands need not be one that each member enthusiastically agrees upon. It may be one which a strong majority agrees upon and with which the others, in love, concur. But if there is one who still, in love, is convicted that the proposed action should not be taken, it cannot in fact be taken.

But this decision for action comes only after the open discussion which follows the 'controlled discussion'. In this open discussion everyone is free to question each other, to elicit further details, to argue the pros and cons of this and that. It may sometimes be felt that a further silence is necessary at a point in the discussion when the company appears to get 'stuck'. It is sometimes helpful in such a silence of a few minutes devotion that each one takes the hand of his neighbour in his own as an act of deeper commitment and renewal of trust. But each company will work out its own way in this as in so many other things, as they best lead to action, to the doing of the Father's will.

One further thing. There are companies of SCK who feel that very much in the way of corporate action cannot be expected of them. They are of two kinds. The first are those companies whose members are really old and realise that actual physical involvement in sheer hard work is beyond them. But 'watchfulness' is not beyond them, nor is the writing of letters. There is a very valuable ministry of the letter and the telephone not only in righting wrongs and procuring action, but in contact with the lonely and those in trouble and despair. In such circumstances a letter or a telephone call can mean a very great deal. The second class consists of those companies whose members are already over-committed and involved either by their professional occupations such as nursing or social work, or in voluntary organisations such as the Samaritans, or in the service of the church. To them again I say that the business of 'watchfulness' is not beyond them; indeed sometimes they are the only people who can point to the need and then it becomes a concern of the company to help to get that need fulfilled, and to be supportive of the members in their work. In so far as such members are trying to do their work as servants of Christ the King, that work becomes a concern of that company of Servants of Christ the King. I say 'a' concern because I am convinced that in an active company concerns may constantly change. If we are attentive to our King and obedient to him I do not think that it is possible for any company to claim that 'our concern is intercession' – or 'evangelism' or whatever. It may be that one or more of such concerns underlies all that we do but we may not limit the direction in which the Lord the Spirit will lead us. We will find that if we are attentive and obedient that the great love and divine compassion will lead us to be his servants in very varied situations and to very varied folk.

BIBLIOGRAPHY AND REFERENCES

Archives

The bulk of the SCK archives has been deposited and is available to researchers at Lambeth Palace Library (LPL). It is intended that further papers will be deposited at LPL in due course. Papers of Archbishop William Temple relating to SCK are stored at WTemple 40 fol. 1-85.

Main references for SCK papers held at LPL:

MS 4808	Central Company record November 1958 to April 1964 and Executive Company record
MS 4809	Executive Company record August 1964 to August 1966
MS 4810	Minutes of the Central and Executive Companies 1966-67
MS 4811	Minutes of the Central and Executive Companies 1967-69
MS 4812	Minutes of the Central and Executive Companies 1969-76
MS 4813	Minutes of the Central and Executive Companies 1976-82 (incomplete)
MS 4814	Minutes of the Central and Executive Companies 1991-95
MS 4815	Miscellaneous correspondence, papers and photographs 1941-1986
MS 4816	Miscellaneous correspondence, papers and photographs 1987-2004
H5013.S25 [Tower]	Issues of the SCK *Newsletter* (variously headed *Newsletter, News Letter, News letter* and SOCKS), together with some Newsletter supplements containing transcriptions of talks given at the annual conference.

Some SCK material is included in the Émile Cammaerts papers in the Senate House Library, University of London (SHL). Professor Cammaerts was a member of the Advisory Group for Christian Cells and a fellow-member with Roger Lloyd at the Athenaeum Club.

Main references for papers relating to SCK and Roger Lloyd held at SHL:

MS800/V/1   Correspondence in English and French between
                 Émile Cammaerts and various correspondents
                 concerning religious and spiritual matters (1927-
                 1953)

MS800/V/2A   Correspondence between Émile Cammaerts and
                 various correspondents concerning religious and
                 spiritual matters, in particular with members of
                 the Advisory Committee for Christian Cells, and
                 with Paul Shuffrey, editor of the 'Church Quarterly
                 Review' (1947-1950)

MS800/V/3   Papers created and/or compiled by Émile
                 Cammaerts, reflecting his interests in the Christian
                 cell movement, and in particular his involvement
                 in a layman capacity with the Advisory Group for
                 Christian Cells (1943-1951)

MS800/V/4   Notes and other papers reflecting Émile Cammaerts'
                 exploration of religious and spiritual matters
                 (c1947-c1952)

Records of the Winchester diocese are held at the Hampshire Record Office. The Winchester Cathedral collection is currently being catalogued. Some articles by Roger Lloyd and one by Émile Cammaerts appeared in diocesan publications which are already in the online catalogue:

44M68/G2   Winchester Diocesan Leaflet (1936-1963)

PER96   The Winchester Churchman, the monthly journal of
                 the Diocese of Winchester (1963-1992)

Roger Lloyd wrote many hundreds of articles which can now be found in the online archives of the *Manchester Guardian*, *The Guardian*, the *Observer*, *The Spectator* and the *Church Times*. Only a few of these make direct mention of SCK. The *Church Times* carried occasional reports of

SCK activities from the 1960s onwards: some of these are included in the bibliography below.

Bibliography

Advisory Group for Christian Cells. (1940). *Draft leaflet*. LPL: Lang 175 fol. 398-404.

An SCK company leader in Bristol. (1947). Letter to a new company leader, dated 11 May 1947. LPL: MS 4815 fol. 59-60.

An SCK company leader in St Vincent. (1974). From St Vincent in the West Indies. SCK *Newsletter*, May 1974, pp. 25-6.

Anon. (1937). Personal impression of the first meeting of the cell. LPL: MS 3234 fol. 321-4.

Anon. (1943). *Waiting upon God*. SCK. LPL: MS 4815 fol. 66-7.

Anon. (1945). *Waiting upon God*. SCK. LPL: MS 4815 fol. 64-5. Reproduced as Part III, Document A.

Anon. (1949). *The Servants of Christ the King*. SCK. SHL: MS800/V/3/4

Anon. (1952). Oxford Conference. SCK *Newsletter*, February 1952, pp. 1-2.

Anon. (1962). *S.C.K.* SCK. LPL: MS 4815 fol. 101-2.

Anon. (1997). Paternoster House. LPL: MS 4816 fol. 120.

Archbishop of York's Conference. (1941). *Malvern, 1941: The Life of the Church and the Order of Society*. London: Longmans, Green and Co.

Archbishop of York's Conference. (1991). *The Malvern Declaration of 1941: the original text together with a commentary by David Arthur*. Industrial Christian Fellowship.

Archbishops' Council. (2009). *Mission-Shaped Church: Church Planting and Fresh Expressions of Church in a Changing Context* (2nd ed.). London: Church House Publishing. ISBN: 978 0 7151 4189 2.

Babington, Richard H. (1963). Company News. SCK *Newsletter*, February 1963, pp. 16-18.

Babington, Richard H. (1963). Waiting upon God. SCK *Newsletter*, Autumn 1963, pp. 1, 4.

Beach, A., & Beach, E. (1981). *Edmund Robert Morgan*. Beach.

Bonhoeffer, Dietrich (1954). *Life Together*. London: SCM Press. ISBN: 978 0 334 00904 7. Originally published as *Gemeinsames Leben* (1939).

Bridge, Brian (1997). *Reflections on the Future of SCK*.SCK.

Bridge, Brian (2008). Revision of 'Adventure in Discipleship'. SCK *Newsletter*, Summer 2008, pp. 10-13.

Bridge, Brian (2013). *Waiting on God: Seeking God's Calling Together in Small Groups*. Cambridge: Grove Books. ISBN: 978-1-85174-874-7.

Brierley, Jim (1969). *What's in a Name?* LPL:MS 4811 fol. 122-3.

Britain Yearly Meeting of the Religious Society of Friends. (2013). *Quaker Faith & Practice* (5th ed.). London: Religious Society of Friends (Quakers) in Britain. ISBN: 978-1-907123-54-2.

Carder, Jill (1973). ... And Began to Speak in Other Tongues. SCK *Newsletter*, May 1973, pp. 3-5.

Church Times. (1988). Priest resigns to become Quaker. *Church Times*, 19 August 1988, p. 1.

Commission on Evangelism. (1945). *Towards the Conversion of England*. Westminster: The Press and Publications Board of the Church Assembly.

Communist International. (1920). Conditions of Admission to the Communist International. Moscow.

Eliot, T. S. (1928). *For Lancelot Andrewes: Essays on Style and Order*. London: Faber and Faber.

Eliot, T. S. (1939). *The Idea of a Christian Society*. London: Faber & Faber.

Eliot, T. S. (1940). *East Coker*.

ffrench-Beytagh, Gonville (1972). *Advice on Waiting upon God*. SCK. Reproduced as Part III, Document C.

ffrench-Beytagh, Gonville (1972). Letter to all Companies.

ffrench-Beytagh, Gonville (1973). *Encountering Darkness*. London: Collins.

ffrench-Beytagh, Gonville (1973). Second Thoughts. SCK *Newsletter*, May 1973, pp. 1-2.

ffrench-Beytagh, Gonville (1978). *Facing Depression*. Oxford: SLG Press. ISBN: 0 7283 0077 X.

ffrench-Beytagh, Gonville, & Hodges, Vera (1986). *A Glimpse of Glory*. London: Darton Longman & Todd. ISBN: 0 232 51691 X.

ffrench-Beytagh, Gonville, & Hodges, Vera (1988). *Tree of Glory*. London: Darton Longman & Todd. ISBN: 0 232 51776 2.

ffrench-Beytagh, Gonville, & Norman, Alison (1975). *Encountering Light*. London: Fontana Books. ISBN: 0006237665.

ffrench-Beytagh, Gonville, & Robinson, Wendy (2010). *Out of the Depths: Encountering Depression* (2nd ed.). Oxford: SLG Press. ISBN: 978-0-7283-0183-2. With an Epilogue by Wendy Robinson.

Godin, Henri, & Daniel, Yvan (1943). *La France - Pays de Mission?* Lyon: Les Éditions de L'Abeille. An edited translation is included in Ward, M. (1949)

Greasley, Jim (1965). SCK Worldwide in 1965? SCK *Newsletter*, March 1965, pp. 6-8.

Hacking, R. D. (1988). *Such a Long Journey: A Biography of Gilbert Shaw, Priest*. Oxford: A. R. Mowbray & Co.

Knight, Eileen (1979). All Hallows' Tottenham SCK Company. SCK *Newsletter (SOCKS)*(23), June 1979, pp. 3-4.

Lloyd, Roger B. (1925). The Industrial Christian Fellowship. *Manchester Guardian*, 8 October 1925, p. 11. In 'Manchester Letters'.

Lloyd, Roger B. (1936). *Crown Him Lord of All: The Story of a Mission in a Lancashire Town*. London: Hodder & Stoughton.

Lloyd, Roger (1937). *The Beloved Community*. London: Nisbet and Co.

Lloyd, Roger (1940). The Way to a Christian Policy. *The Spectator*, 23 February 1940, pp. 241-2.

Lloyd, Roger (1941). Notes for Winchester Fellowship. Winchester. LPL:MS 4815 fol. 2.

Lloyd, Roger (1942). *A Design for an Active Religious Order of Anglican Laity for the Purpose of Providing the Church of England with an Organised and Disciplined Body of Witnesses*. Winchester. LPL: WTemple 40 fol. 2-5. (short title: *Design for an Order*)

Lloyd, Roger (1942). Covering letter sent with *Design for an Order*. Winchester. LPL: WTemple 40 fol. 1.

Lloyd, Roger (1944). SCK *Newsletter*, January 1944.

Lloyd, Roger (1944). *The Inspiration of God*. London: Geoffrey Bles: The Centenary Press.

Lloyd, Roger (1945). Cancellation of Conference. SCK *Newsletter*, January 1945, pp. 1-3.

Lloyd, Roger (1947). SCK *Newsletter*, June 1947.

Lloyd, Roger (1948). SCK *Newsletter*, Epiphany 1948.

Lloyd, Roger (1949). The Cell Movement and the Servants of Christ the King. ACS *Newsletter*, pp. 34-6. (ACS = Additional Curates Society)

Lloyd, Roger (1951). The Future of SCK. SCK *Newsletter*, May 1951, pp. 2-3.

Lloyd, Roger (1952). Message from the Warden. SCK *Newsletter*, February 1952, pp. 2-4.

Lloyd, Roger (1952). *The Church and the Artisan Today*. London: Longmans, Green and Co.

Lloyd, Roger (1953). *An Adventure in Discipleship: The Servants of Christ the King*. London: Longmans, Green and Co.

Lloyd, Roger (1955). Is SCK Excessively Spiritual? SCK *Newsletter*, February 1955, pp. 4-7.

Lloyd, Roger (1955). Why SCK Companies Must Have a Rule of Life. SCK *Newsletter*, June 1955, pp. 4-6.

Lloyd, Roger (1957). But What Do These Companies Actually Do? SCK *Newsletter*, February 1957, pp. 4-8.

Lloyd, Roger (1957). Vocation in SCK. SCK *Newsletter*, October 1957, pp. 6-11.

Lloyd, Roger (1963). Chapters from an Unwritten History. SCK *Newsletter*, February 1963, pp. 1-13.

Lloyd, Roger (1966). *The Church of England 1900-1965: A Meditation on an Historical Theme*. London: SCM Press.

Mason, Alistair (1993). *History of the Society of the Sacred Mission*. Norwich: Canterbury Press. ISBN: 1-85311-079-5.

Milligan, Edward (1948). Quaker Service. *Friends Quarterly*, April 1948.

Morgan, Edmund R. (1944). Waiting upon God: An Explanation. SCK. Reproduced as Part III, Document B.

Morgan, Edmund R. (1963). *Reginald Somerset Ward: His Life and Letters*. Oxford: A. R. Mowbray & Co.

Morgan, Edmund R., & Lloyd, Roger (1948). *The Mission of the Anglican Communion*. London: SPCK and SPG.

Murry, John Middleton (1939). *The Price of Leadership*. London: SCM Press.

Newman, John Henry (1893). *Meditations and Devotions of the Late Cardinal Newman*. London: Longmans Green & Co. Meditation dated 7 March 1848.

Norman, Alison (1964). SCK *Newsletter*, May 1964, pp. 4-7.

Norman, Alison (1964). Servants of Christ the King: Companies to be Open to All Christians. *Church Times*, 11 September 1964, p. 3.

Norman, Alison (1969). Impressions of the Open Meeting. SCK *Newsletter*, May 1969, pp. 8-10.

Norman, Alison (1974). Pilgrim's report. SCK *Newsletter*, May 1974, pp. 5-24.

Norman, Alison (1975). Thirty-Six Hours. SCK *Newsletter*, February 1975, pp. 7-16.

Norman, Alison (1989). A New Warden. SCK *Newsletter*(60), August 1989, p. 2.

Norman, Alison (2007-08). Anthology of SCK members' lives. Unpublished.

Norman, Alison (2009). *Snapshot of SCK in 2007-08*. SCK.

Norman, Alison (2014). Tributes to Wendy Robinson. SCK *Newsletter*(131), Summer 2014, pp. 1-4.

Norman, Alison (2014). The 2014 Conference. SCK *Newsletter*(132), Winter 2014, pp. 1-3.

Parker, Olive (1962). *The New Commandment: The Servants of Christ the King*. London: Darton, Longman & Todd.

Parker, Olive (1963). An Essay in Self-Examination. SCK *Newsletter*, Autumn 1963, pp. 5-8.

Parker, Olive (1964). Call to Commitment. SCK *Newsletter*, October 1964, pp. 5-10.

Parker, Olive (1966). SCK *Newsletter*, October 1966.

[Parker, Olive] (c. 1966). *Structure of SCK*.

Parsloe, Guy (1971). SCK: A Meditation on Essentials. SCK *Newsletter*, November 1971, pp. 2-10.

Robinson, Wendy (1974). Exploring Silence. SCK *Newsletter*, January 1974, pp. 2-17.

Robinson, Wendy (1995). *The Lost Traveller's Dream: Developing a theology for working with mental illness*. Oxford: Oxford Christian Institute for Counselling. ISBN: 1-899835-00-8.

Robinson, Wendy (2007). *A Journey to the Russian Orthodox Church*. SCK.

Robinson, Wendy (2013). *Exploring Silence* (3rd ed.). Oxford: Fairacres Publications. ISBN: 978-0-7283-0237-2.

Robinson, Wendy, Norman, Alison, & Bridge, Brian (2013). Waiting upon God for the Future. SCK *Newsletter*(127), Spring 2013, p. 3.

Rudd, Julian (1960). The Application of the SCK Rule. SCK *Newsletter*, Winchester Conference 1960, pp. 4-12.

SCK. (1952). Holding the Companies Together. SCK *Newsletter*, February 1952, pp. 4-? (pages after p. 4 are missing in the archive copy).

SCK. (1954). Adventure in Discipleship: The SCK Book. SCK *Newsletter*, February 1954, pp. 3-5.

SCK. (1958). SCK Conference July 29th to August 5th 1958. SCK *Newsletter*, February 1958, pp. 5-6.

SCK. (1960). *In Company Together*. SCK. LPL: MS 4815 fol. 77-80.

SCK. (1964). The Regional Spirit. SCK *Newsletter*, February 1964, pp. 6-10.

SCK. (1979). Other Company News. SCK *Newsletter (*SOCKS*)*(23), June 1979, p. 5.

SCK. (1997). Central Company. SCK *Newsletter*, April 1997, p. 7.

SCK Central Company. (1959). SCK *Newsletter*, November 1959.

SCK Central Company. (1959). Minutes. LPL: MS 4808 fol. 15.

SCK Central Company. (1960). Minutes. 9-11 November 1960. LPL:MS 4808 fol. 26v.

SCK Central Company. (1964). Policy Statement and Recommendations. SCK *Newsletter*, October 1964, pp. 11-12.

SCK Central Company. (1969). Conference. SCK *Newsletter*, May 1969, pp. 11-13.

SCK Central Company. (1979). Minutes. 8 May 1979. LPL:MS 4813 fol. 39.

SCK Central Company. (1982). Minutes. 23 February 1982. LPL:MS 4813 fol. 76.

SCK Central Company Paper. (c. 1972). The Promise or Rule. LPL:MS 4812 pp. 160-1.

SCK Conference. (1943). *An Order for Anglican Laypeople*. LPL: WTemple 40 fol. 24-6.

SCK Conference. (1948). Letter to all Companies and Advisers. August 1948. Quoted in full by Roger Lloyd in *An Adventure in Discipleship* (1953) pp. 102-106.

SCK Conference. (1951). The St Swithun's Conference August 3-10, 1951. SCK *Newsletter*, October 1951, pp. 1-5.

SCK Conference. (1994). Waiting upon God. SCK *Newsletter*(73), July 1994, pp. 8-9.

SCK Conference. (1997). The Future of SCK: Conference Decisions. SCK *Newsletter*(82), September 1997, p. 22.

Sister Anne Julian CSMV (2002). 59th Annual Conference. SCK *Newsletter*(96), Summer 2002, pp. 2-7.

Sister Anne Julian CSMV (2007). Warden's Letter. SCK *Newsletter*(109), January 2007, pp. 1-2.

Sister Anne Julian CSMV (2008). Warden SCK. SCK *Newsletter*(113), Lent 2008, pp. 3-4.

Smyly, W. (2006). Conference 2006. SCK *Newsletter*, Summer 2006, pp. 2-3.

Stevenson, Pauline (2000). *Groups for Silence in and out of Psychiatry*. September 2000. Paper given at the Special Interest Group in Spirituality of the Royal College of Psychiatrists, September 2000.

Thom, Kennedy (1979). And a company goes on to another kind of life. SCK *Newsletter (SOCKS)*(24), September 1979, pp. 5-6.

Thorburn, Austin (1994). Draft letter to church leaders. July 1994.

Thorburn, Austin (1998). Is SCK a Movement? SCK *Newsletter*(84), June 1998, pp. 19-20.

Thorburn, Austin (1999). *Reflections on the Benedictine Rule*. SCK.

Thorburn, Peter (1990). What is SCK? SCK.

Verney, Stephen (2010). *Fire in Coventry* (new ed.). Coventry: Diocese of Coventry. ISBN: 978-0-9565607-0-4.

Vincent, John (Ed.) (2011). *Christian Communities*. Sheffield: Ashram Press. ISBN: 978-0-9559073-2-6.

Ward, Maisie (1949). *France Pagan? The Mission of Abbé Godin*. London: Sheed & Ward. Includes an edited translation of Godin & Daniel (1943).

Ward, Reginald Somerset (1937). *A Fellowship in the Gospel*. LPL:MS 2946 fol. 23-9.

[Ward, Reginald Somerset] (1937). *The Cell*. LPL:MS 2946 fol. 16-21.

Willis, George (1968). Areas of Questioning. SCK *Newsletter*, January 1968, pp. 1-4.

Wyon, Olive (1963). *Living Springs: New Religious Movements in Western Europe*. London: SCM Press.

INDEX

ecumenical companies 27–8, 31–2, 47, 110
Ecumenical Renewal Group 38
Eliot, T. S. 5
environmental concerns 27
Epiphany conference (1944) 12–13
evangelism 75–8
  biblical context 79–80
  in England (1940s) 2–3
  as obligation 9, 14, 21
evangelistic methods 77, 80–1
Executive Company 93, 105, 107
'explode into action' 72, 133
Exploring Silence (Robinson, 2013) 52

Fellowship in the Gospel *see* First Cell
Fellowship of Contemplative Prayer (FCP) 43, 46–7
fellowship of fellowships 105–8, 111
feminism 27
ffrench-Beytagh, Gonville 18, 35
  on growth of SCK 42–3
  influence on SCK 107
  on unanimity 88
  vision for SCK 40–1
  on waiting on God 72
First Cell 7, 59, 60
founding conference (1943) 7–8
Fountain Trust 27, 135–6

General Rule 23, 109–11, 112
Grimes, John 1, 15

Hammersley, John 39
Hampshire conference (2014) 54
Harper, Michael 27
Haswell, Pauline 18, 96
Hodges, H. A. 6
Holy Spirit 63–4, 91
  'anxiety of the Holy Ghost' 70, 72
  fellowship of 129
  freedom in 105
  workings in small groups 87
homosexuality 26
Honest to God (Robinson, 1963) 27
Horneck, Anthony 84
hothouse atmospheres 86
Hubback, George 109

Idea of a Christian Society, The (Eliot, 1939) 2, 4–5
In Company Together (SCK, 1960) 20
Industrial Christian Fellowship 5, 75
Inspiration of God, The (Lloyd, 1944) 12, 91
Ipswich experience 20–1, 78